Assessment in Practice
Raising standards in secondary geography

Photo: Margaret Roberts
Department of Educational Studies
University of Sheffield

Assessment in Practice

Raising standards in secondary geography

Geographical
Association

Editors John Hopkin, Steve Telfer and Graham Butt

Acknowledgements

The authors and editors would also like to thank the following individuals
and organisations for their valuable contributions to this book:

Members of the Herefordshire Geography Teachers' Group, especially Karen Pape and Mike Hallett
Assessment Team, Birmingham Advisory and Support Service
Robert Gilbert, Bishop Luffa School, West Sussex
John Kyrle High School
Shenley Court School, Birmingham

© the Geographical Association, 2000

ISBN 1 899085 78 5
First published 2000
Impression number 10 9 8 7 6 5 4 3 2 1
Year 2003 2002 2001

Published by the Geographical Association, 160 Solly Street, Sheffield S1 4BF.
The Geographical Association is a registered charity: no 313129.

The Publications Officer of the GA would be happy to hear from other potential authors who have
ideas for geography books. You may contact the Officer via the GA at the address above.

Sub edited by Kath Davies
Designed and typeset in England by ATG Design,
Catalyst Creative Imaging, Leeds
Printed and bound in England by Amadeus Press, Huddersfield

Contents

Foreword *David Lambert*
Introduction *John Hopkin*

Foreword

This book is the result of the sustained effort of the Assessment and Examinations Working Group of the Geographical Association over a period of some years. It represents a considerable advance from *Assessment Works* by Butt *et al.* (1995), which offered an immediate and helpful framework for thinking about assessment following the publication of the Dearing Review of the National Curriculum in the same year.

Assessment in Practice builds on a number of useful distinctions outlined in the earlier publication, notably that between formative and summative assessment practice. For example, different emphases, purposes and practices are distinguished between 'day-to-day', 'medium-term' and 'long-term' assessment needs and strategies. It also emphasises the role of assessment in raising standards in geography. Lots of practical examples and illustrations are presented which lead to a discussion of departmental policy making for assessment.

All in all this is an essential book for the departmental professional library and for all geography 'subject leaders'.

David Lambert
January 2000

Contributors

This book is the result of team effort on the part of the authors and editors; who are members of the Geographical Association's Assessment and Examinations Working Group.

David Balderstone is a Lecturer in Geography Education at the
University of London, Institute of Education.

Dr. Graham Butt is Senior Lecturer in Geographical Education at the University of Birmingham.

Emma Flinders teaches geography at King Charles I School, Kidderminster.

Keith Flinders was formerly head of geography, The Grange School, Stourbridge.

Dr. John Hopkin is Chair of the AEWG and works for Birmingham Advisory and Support Service.

Nic Howes is Head of Geography at the John Kyrle High School, Ross-on-Wye.

Dr. David Lambert is former chair of the AEWG and Reader in Education at the University of London, Institute of Education and Publications Officer of the GA 1996-2000.

Steve Telfer is an Adviser with the West Sussex Advisory and Inspection Service.

Contributions from other AEWG members: Terri Collins, Mike Gorman, Sarah Green, Pat Hutchings, Jill Jackson, John Kenyon, Luke Magee, Mike Milton, Bob Pike, Alan Waters and Dr. Phil Wood.

Introduction

Assessment has always been an integral part of teaching and learning, and good practice in assessment is an important means of improving students' attainment. However, since the introduction of the National Curriculum in England and Wales, attention has focused at a national level on summative assessment and the use of assessment data to report results, compare schools' performance and set targets (Black and Wiliam, 1998). For example, geography teachers have received extensive support from SCAA/QCA and from ACAC/ACCAC in making level judgements, but less in improving formative assessment. The distinction is between assessment *of* learning, and assessment *for* learning (James, 1998).

This book is a practical manual designed to help geography teachers and departments to review and improve their assessment, and so raise standards in geography. Chapter 1, by David Balderstone, sets out some of the central issues in assessment and discusses the importance of good, consistent professional judgements about students' attainments. In Chapter 2, Graham Butt focuses on the purposes of assessment and some of the tensions between the different types of assessment, emphasising the key role of formative assessment in helping to ensure 'better feedback both to students, in what they must do to improve, and to teachers, to inform forward planning' (Ofsted, 1999).

In Chapter 3, John Hopkin and Steve Telfer establish the links between assessment and progression in geography. They argue that assessment *for* learning and assessment *of* learning need to be approached differently, and at different times in the teaching cycle, and that teachers can improve their practice by being clear about how and when these are best used. This chapter is at the heart of *Assessment in Practice*, setting out a model of short-, medium- and long-term assessment strategies and purposes which are amplified in subsequent chapters.

Chapter 4, by John Hopkin, covers short-term assessment. This is the most important focus for attention because it is integral to day-to-day teaching and learning and is firmly centred on formative assessment, which both provides opportunities for students to improve their work, and gives teachers feedback to help them adjust their plans. Nic Howes shows in Chapter 5 how medium-term assessment helps draw together or 'anchor' the professional judgements made from regular classroom interactions. Nic provides a wealth of first-hand examples of how key enquiries can provide good evidence of students' capabilities and make assessment more systematic. Medium-term assessment can be partly formative, by setting targets for students; however it also makes an important contribution to the process of developing geography portfolios.

It is this long-term aspect of assessment which is developed in Chapter 6; here Nic sets out the purposes of portfolios and their key role in making judgements about attainment, and offers some practical suggestions for improvement. Further aspects of long-term assessment are dealt with in Chapter 7. Here Keith and Emma Flinders outline good practice in setting successful departmental examinations, so as to ensure that they provide a positive experience for students and useful information for teachers, and on making best use of the Examiner's Report to raise standards at GCSE. The chapter concludes with an overview of target setting, pointing out the importance of a good system of assessment to target *getting*. Chapter 8, by John Hopkin, draws together the arguments and strategies developed through *Assessment in Practice* with advice on assessment policy.

Each chapter concludes with a number of professional development activities; these relate specifically to the material in that chapter, but taken together from a comprehensive continuous professional development programme for improving assessment in geography at secondary level.

Photo: Margaret Roberts, Department of
Educational Studies, University of Sheffield

Chapter 1

Beyond testing? Issues for teacher assessment in geography

'Teacher assessment is fundamental to good teaching. By making assessments during the key stage, you will build up your knowledge of individual students' strengths and weaknesses, which will help you plan your teaching. By making judgements at the end of the key stage on students' performance against the level descriptions set out in the National Curriculum Orders, you will provide important information for students, their parents and your colleagues' (Dearing, 1996, p. i).

Introduction

Assessment has always been an integral part of teaching and learning. We would all accept that the 'educational' purpose of teacher assessment is to help young people to progress in their learning in geography. Implementing the assessment requirements of the National Curriculum in Geography is now a professional matter. It is reassuring to be reminded by Rawling and Westaway that:

'it is the teacher who is best placed to draw together knowledge about a student's performance and to balance strengths and weaknesses to reach a sound professional decision' (Rawling and Westaway, 1996, p. 128).

The role and purpose of assessment is considered in general terms in Chapter 2, which seeks to address the fundamental question 'Why do we assess?', as

well as outlining some of the principles upon which the national curriculum assessment system is based.

There is, however, a tension between the formative role of assessment and the need to provide a summative assessment of students' achievement in geography. This is especially so at key stage 3, which leads us to consider some broader issues relating to the use of level descriptions which are central to the system of formal assessment of national curriculum geography.

> **The main questions raised in this first chapter are:**
>
> - **can we reach agreement about these judgements within departments and amongst schools?**
> - **will it be possible to identify 'national standards' using level descriptions for summative assessment?**
> - **how can the process of 'levelling' help us to develop our professional understanding of achievement and standards in geography?**
> - **how can teacher assessment influence teaching and learning in geography in a positive way?**

The first two questions relate to issues about the reliability of the judgements that are being made. It has always been the view of the GA Assessment and Examination Working Group that 'traditional' concerns about reliability (or 'national standards') should not distort the quality of assessment practice (Butt *et al.*, 1995). Teachers have more realistic and practical concerns about the consistency and fairness of the assessments that they are making.

Can we agree about judgements?

Concerns that teachers may have about whether their judgements are consistent with those of others (within departments and amongst schools) may be difficult to resolve to everyone's satisfaction. It is unlikely that teacher assessment will ever produce unambiguous national standards, as teachers within schools base the whole system upon trusted professional judgements. However, this can in itself be regarded as a strength of the system.

If teacher assessment is to be seen as dependable and is to gain public credibility, there will need to be some degree of consistency between schools and teachers in the judgements that are being made (Gipps, 1994; Lambert, 1997). Teachers' knowledge of the level descriptions, and understanding of what they mean in relation to students' work, will increase with experience. One of the most effective ways of gaining this experience is to discuss students' work and achievements with other teachers. This, together with reaching agreement about what evidence we might expect to find of progress through the levels, is the approach to take.

The development of a **school** or **department portfolio** of selected pieces of students' work is of crucial importance in the assessment process; it is described in detail in Chapter 6. These **'Level portfolios'** will exemplify the agreed assessment standards within a school and will provide the 'benchmarks' against which the levels achieved by all students can be judged. The compilation of these portfolios should be approached in a manageable and developmental way. We should remember that 'there is no statutory requirement to keep detailed records or evidence on every student' (Dearing, 1996, p. i).

Teachers need to adopt a 'critical' approach in the process of reaching agreement about what exemplifies attainment at each level. It is unlikely that we will reach rapid and easy consensus. However, the actual process of arguing about what constitutes attainment at a particular Level and what should be included in a portfolio can be vital in helping teachers to begin to develop and share an understanding of progress (Lambert, 1997).

To ensure that these discussions are meaningful and manageable, only a small sample of different students' work should be selected for discussion and agreement about attainment in relation to the level descriptions. It is essential that all teachers involved in teaching through the key stage participate in these discussions. We can then apply the understanding that we develop through this process when making Level judgements about the attainment of all students.

These discussions should also look at the **'contexts'** in which the assessed work was produced, including the resources used in the learning activities and the strategies used to elicit responses from the students. This will enable us to take account of a wide range of assessment evidence (including oral responses). This **context description** is an essential part of the process of reaching agreement about standards.

It is very unlikely that there will ever be a network of local or regional moderators to help teachers to validate their judgements. Where possible, teachers could take advantage of opportunities provided by the Geographical Association, local education authorities and other in-service training providers to discuss examples of 'Level portfolios' with colleagues from other schools.

Can we identify 'national standards' using level descriptions for summative assessment?

To develop any acceptable notion of 'national standards', we must view teacher assessment using an entirely new approach. This model, or system, is often referred to as **educational assessment** and it requires us to develop a different view of the concept of 'reliability' in assessment. Gipps (1994) has proposed an alternative framework of guiding principles, or 'criteria of quality in educational assessment', to support the development of teacher assessment. This includes the idea of **comparability**, which is less rigid and restrictive than that of reliability. Teachers can achieve it through the consistency of approach and a common understanding of assessment criteria (i.e. the level descriptions). This is therefore a 'professional', rather than a 'technical' or 'bureaucratic' approach to assessment.

It will take time for teachers to develop their expertise and understanding. However, there is a considerable amount of useful support material available to help teachers build up increasingly consistent standards. The *Exemplification of Standards* booklets produced by SCAA (now QCA) (1996a) and ACAC (now ACCAC)(1996) are designed to help teachers to make these judgements about standards. The use of the *Optional Tests and Tasks* (SCAA, 1996b; ACAC, 1997) has also helped to standardise expectations within and amongst schools (Tidmarsh and Weeden, 1997).

Can the levelling process help develop our professional understanding of standards in geography?

Before the introduction of the National Curriculum in Geography and teacher assessment, we had only a very limited understanding about what constituted levels of attainment (or standards) in geography in key stages 1-3, although we have learned much from using GCSE criteria at 14-16. Approaches to planning for progression had been developed but teachers probably had only a limited understanding of what evidence of progression actually looked like in practice. Now that the national curriculum is established, we have a much clearer route-map to guide progression and attainment.

Teachers talking to each other, comparing portfolios of students' work and agreeing amongst themselves

about progress through the Levels is certainly the way forward. The use of level descriptions will help us to develop a better understanding of progression through different levels of attainment in geography.

The example, 'Making judgements about Julia's work' (Figure 1 overleaf), provided by Rawling and Westaway (1996) has proved a useful starting point for teachers' discussions about the 'process of making judgements'. The accompanying comments (shown below) are particularly useful as they illustrate how we might arrive at a judgement about performance.

Summary and judgement about Julia's performance

In making a decision about Julia's performance, her teacher considered Levels 5, 6 and 7. Level 6 was judged to be the 'best fit' (Figure 1).

The small amount of work presented here covers several aspects of geography, although environmental issues are now well represented. However, the piece of work on acid rain in SCAA, 1996a, pages 28-29, was also completed by Julia and may be considered alongside this portfolio. Her teacher knows far more about Julia's work than can be included here; in particular she has evidence of Julia's work on other topics and knows that she is a capable participant in group activities and fieldwork.

The work presented here shows Julia working at local, regional and national scales and, in particular, 'Should we stay or go' and 'Household spending' reveal that Julia is capable of making connections across scales (village to larger town; village to nation).

In 'Should we stay or go', Julia has developed ideas from the textbook to draw a diagram which effectively summarises the reasons for rural to urban migration. In this she demonstrates characteristics of Level 6 by describing how processes operating at different scales (family, village, town) create geographical patterns and contribute to change in places.

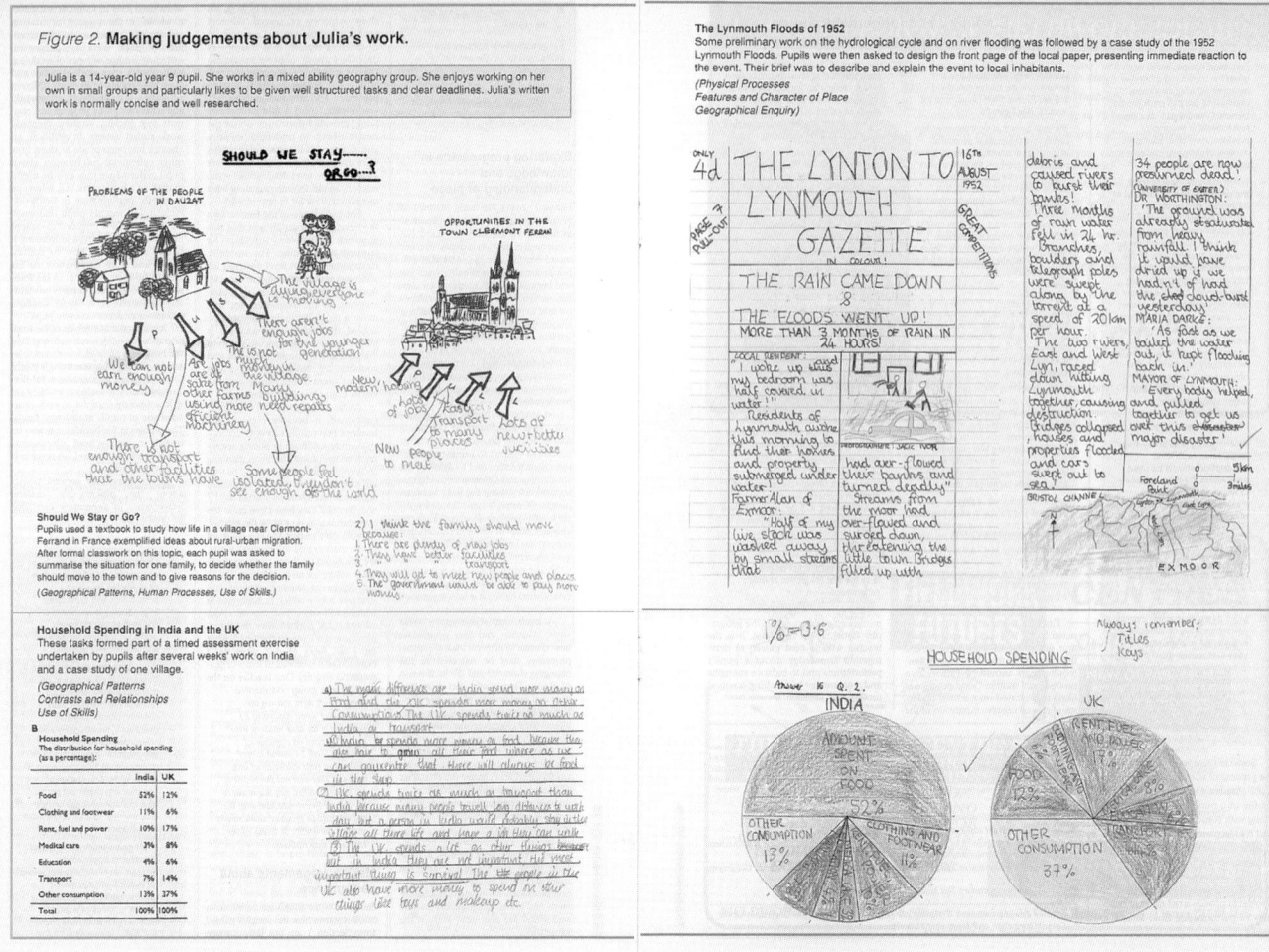

Figure 1: Making judgements about Julia's work. Source: Rawling and Westaway, 1996.

Julia's understanding of physical processes and the way in which they affect patterns and places is revealed in the Lynmouth floods exercise in an interesting way. By using the views and opinions of local residents alongside the more factual explanation in the newspaper article, Julia shows that she has moved beyond making a simple link between cause and consequence in physical geography (Level 5), and appreciate that different aspects of environmental change have different effects on people and places (Level 6). The exercise did not give her an opportunity to extend the work in this direction.

The work on 'Household spending' is competent. Julia has used the required technique (pie charts) accurately (characteristic of Level 5) and has drawn conclusions consistent with the evidence. The question did not allow a choice of technique. Although her answer displays some confusion between absolute amounts and proportions, nevertheless the explanations are sound (emphasis on 'survival' in India; wider range of consumption in UK) and demonstrate understanding of the link between ways of life and patterns of spending (typical of Level 6).

Overall these pieces of work reveal that Julia is competent in applying skills and understanding in structured enquiry work (typical of Level 6) and, when given the opportunity, she is capable of some degree of independence in identifying questions and planning her own investigations (e.g. the structure of the newspaper article). Her teacher realises that she may be ready for greater challenge in this respect.

Although demonstrating the ability to explain human and physical processes and to make links between the features and character of places, Julia is not yet able to produce work with the depth of analysis and appreciation of interactions which would suggest performance at Level 7. There has not been opportunity for Julia to show consideration of the global scale. On balance, *her teacher judges Level 6 to be the best description of Julia's performance.*

The examples of students' work illustrating 'characteristics of aspects of performance' at a variety of Level bands in Section 1 of the *Exemplification of Standards* (Dearing, 1996) can perform a similar function. However, they also illustrate the difficulty of applying any part or whole of the level descriptions to individual pieces of students' work.

There are limitations within the level descriptions and there is not yet enough evidence to show whether they correspond realistically to the nature of students' progress in geography. Butt *et al.* (1995) point out that some aspects of progression in the level descriptions are debatable. For example, it is wrong to assume that many students working at Level 3 could not 'begin to explain geographical patterns and physical and human processes', which is part of the Level 5 description.

> *'These explanations may be partial and incomplete but they are simple explanations concurrent with the students' age, experience, intellectual capacity and the context in which geographical learning has taken place'* (Butt *et al.*, 1995, p. 89).

It follows that if the level descriptions are flawed, so too will be the judgements based on them. Butt *et al.* acknowledge that this problem is one of interpretation: 'Could "explanations" expected at Level 5 by some teachers, actually be the same as the "descriptions" required at Level 3 by others?' (Butt *et al.*, 1995, p. 89).

The need to interpret level descriptions could be seen as one of their strengths as it provides teachers with opportunities to apply professional judgements. There is little evidence from research to show how children progress through their geographical education. While this continues to be the case, we will continue to rely on the materials and examples provided by SCAA/QCA and ACAC/ACCAC to help us to resolve these issues.

Can teacher assessment influence teaching and learning positively?

The department or school portfolio of students' work can play a key role in this system of 'educational assessment' outlined in this book and in the development of the geography curriculum in schools. As well as supporting teachers making judgements about students' achievements in geography, it can perform an effective 'monitoring' function. It will reflect the standards of achievement in geography in a school. The portfolio can also be used to monitor 'curriculum coverage' as it will reflect the curriculum experience of students in geography.

An important question for teachers and departments to ask will be: Can this experience enable students to demonstrate positive achievement (i.e. what they know, understand and can do)? Teachers may then consider whether their school's geography curriculum provides opportunities for students to reach higher levels of attainment. For example, do students have opportunities to demonstrate 'independence in posing appropriate questions, planning investigations and providing articulate and substantiated arguments' (Geographical Enquiry from Rawling and Westaway, 1996, p. 125).

Such considerations can feed into planning for the geography curriculum (Chapters 3 and 4). Understanding what the level descriptions and programmes of study tell us about progression and expectations in geography should also help us to make 'sound decisions about curriculum and assessment planning' (Rawling and Westaway, 1996, p. 125). Most schools have spent considerable time adapting and developing the taught curriculum, whereas Ofsted's (1996) study of findings from the 1994-95 inspection of geography found that, in many schools, assessment was insufficiently integrated into planning. Figure 2 shows how assessment can be integrated into the planning process.

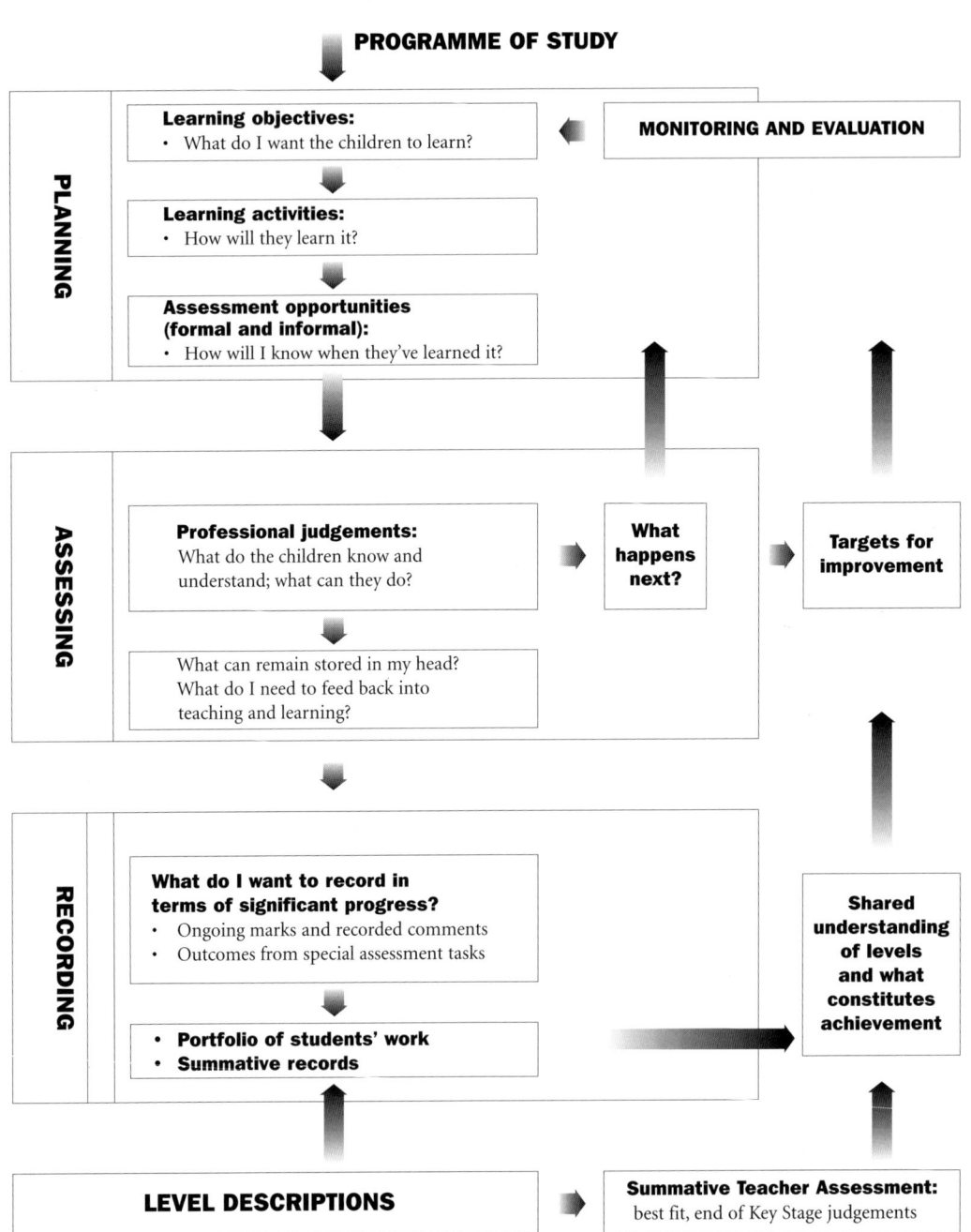

PROGRAMME OF STUDY

PLANNING

Learning objectives:
• What do I want the children to learn?

MONITORING AND EVALUATION

Learning activities:
• How will they learn it?

Assessment opportunities (formal and informal):
• How will I know when they've learned it?

ASSESSING

Professional judgements:
What do the children know and understand; what can they do?

What happens next?

Targets for improvement

What can remain stored in my head? What do I need to feed back into teaching and learning?

RECORDING

What do I want to record in terms of significant progress?
• Ongoing marks and recorded comments
• Outcomes from special assessment tasks

Shared understanding of levels and what constitutes achievement

• **Portfolio of students' work**
• **Summative records**

LEVEL DESCRIPTIONS

Summative Teacher Assessment: best fit, end of Key Stage judgements

Figure 2: Assessment in the Geography National Curriculum. Adapted from: Butt *et al.,* 1995.

Evaluation and day-to-day assessment of student progress has often been identified as a relatively weak feature of geographical education in secondary schools (Ofsted, 1995; Butt and Smith, 1998). However, by developing an understanding of the level descriptions, teachers can improve their own formative assessment. As we mark students' work and discuss the marking with students, we can use this understanding to make more informative comments about their progress and future targets. Marking and target setting in geography will become more meaningful and purposeful, and assessment will have a positive impact on learning.

There are other implications for assessment practice. The benefits of an 'educational model' of teacher assessment are unlikely to be realised under a departmental assessment system that is dependent on standardised end-of-unit tests (Lambert, 1997). A quest for the most 'reliable' methods of assessment could limit curriculum development and innovation in teaching and learning in geography. Rigidly following an assessment scheme linked to a textbook might also be limiting, as well as possibly removing the opportunity for teachers to develop their understanding of progression and attainment in geography.

The *Optional Tests and Tasks* (SCAA, 1996b; ACAC, 1997) can perform a variety of functions. They can be used to provide additional assessment evidence or to assist teachers when making judgements. The detailed marking schemes/assessment criteria can also help us to develop an understanding of progression when used with examples of students' work. They may represent the 'state of the art' in assessment practice as they display many of the desirable qualities of assessment tasks that we have argued for in the past (Balderstone and Lambert, 1992; Butt *et al.*, 1995). Teachers are already using them as models from which to develop their own assessment tasks and mark schemes (Chapter 5). Together the SCAA and ACAC materials provide us with a variety of examples of tasks that can be used to gather evidence about students' achievement in geography.

Summary

The language and rhetoric coming from the centre in recent times has certainly been a lot more helpful and respectful of teachers' professionalism. SCAA (now QCA) proposed looking for 'effective and manageable approaches for promoting consistency in teacher assessment' (SCAA, 1996a, p. i). Geography teachers are now developing 'Level portfolios' of students' work to exemplify attainment in geography in their schools and to help them to make judgements about the overall performance of individual students.

Photo: Jacky Chapman/Format.

Chapter 2

Teaching, learning and assessment overview

- **What role does assessment play in the teaching and learning of geography?**
- **Why should we assess?**

The main issues explored within this chapter are that:

- **students are at the centre of the assessment process;**
- **the cornerstone of assessment is the making of professional judgements about students' work;**
- **assessment can fulfil a number of purposes, but the balance amongst these purposes varies over time;**
- **different types of assessment can serve educational and/or bureaucratic needs;**
- **the National Curriculum for Geography uses an assessment based on level descriptions.**

Introduction

The theme running through this book is 'assessment working' for professional development and for raising student achievement. Assessment has become a focal part of the teachers' professional role following the implementation of the Education Reform Act of 1988 and the creation of the national curriculum. Interestingly, until the passing of this Act the government of the day had perceived neither the school curriculum nor its assessment as central to its sphere of educational influence, preferring to leave both in the hands of the profession. The introduction of the national curriculum changed this *status quo* by specifying in detail what should be taught, and by focusing increasingly on raising attainment.

The last decade has also seen a shift in the relationship between public examinations and teacher assessment. The need for good, regularly-produced assessment information to inform teachers about student progress, aid lesson planning and evaluation, and help in making professional judgements about student attainment is now almost universally recognised. Teacher assessments have become a major component of educational practice, helping students to improve their attainment within each key stage of the National Curriculum for Geography and us to make decisions about student attainment. Teacher assessment is now pivotal to the overall planning, organisation and recording of learning.

However, teacher assessment is not unproblematic. This is partly because it serves both educational and bureaucratic purposes. Since the 1995 revision to the national curriculum, summative teacher assessment has had to be publicly reported at the end of key stage 3. As a result, the consistency of *standards,* across schools and even amongst individual teachers in the same schools, has become an issue.

The national curriculum brought a new emphasis on teacher assessment, now seen as central to the process of enabling students to improve their attainment in geography. Regular, reliable information on student achievement is needed, to meet student needs, plan future learning effectively (formative teacher assessment), and improve the basis for judging a student's level of attainment effectively at the end-of-key stage (summative teacher assessment). Teacher assessment is the key to evaluating teaching and developing students' understanding of how to improve their performance in geography.

Why do we assess?

The purposes of assessment in many schools (some might say within the entire education system) have

gone largely unchallenged for years. In this respect, the national curriculum can be seen as a useful 'agent of change'. The revised curriculum introduced a model for the national assessment of students aged from 5 to 16 within a framework of attainment targets, statements of attainment and Levels. This raised fundamental assessment questions. The ideas formulated by the Task Group for Assessment and Testing (TGAT 1988) were partially revised in 1995 with the creation of level descriptions, which were modified slightly in Curriculum 2000. The concept of 'best fit' performance by students, measured against these level descriptions, removed some of the complexities of the initial assessment model, although it left firmly in place the 'theory' of level criteria independent of age. However, the fundamental question about *why* we assess remained unanswered, and specifically the part played by marking, special assessment tasks, tests and other strategies in the wider process of teacher assessment.

Assessment by teachers or awarding bodies has traditionally been seen as 'an inevitable and essential

Some assessment terminology

Certification. The provision of an award, usually as a paper qualification, for performance in given assessment(s).

Evaluation. The use of assessment information to appraise some aspect of the teaching and learning process. This might be an appraisal of the assessment task itself, of the teaching previously carried out, or of the learning that has resulted as witnessed by assessment results.

Informal assessment. Part of the classroom routine, for example, observing students as they work, questioning them or through discussion.

Formal assessment. An 'occasion' set up internally or externally. Examples would range from a short test or special assessment task to public examinations.

Formative assessment. Using formally or informally collected information about students' learning to plan and support future learning.

Summative assessment. Using assessment information, usually from a variety of tasks, to produce a statement of what a student knows, understands and can do.

Teacher assessment. The continuing process of assessment through which teachers monitor and record student progress. The information gathered is used both to support future student learning and eventually to make a summative judgement of student progress. At key stage 3, judgements about national curriculum levels are based on teacher assessment.

part of the education process' (Lambert, 1997, p.255). It has summative, formative, certification and evaluative roles (Harlen *et al.,* 1992) (see below for a brief explanation of each of these and other terms used within the context of assessment).

Assessment is often thought of as a 'one-way' process, with the teacher or examiner as 'assessor' and the student as passive recipient of a judgement about his or her attainment. 'Two-way' models of assessment, are much more helpful, involving discussions between students and teachers about the assessment information gathered and the next steps in the learning process. Here we are finding out about the student as a learner of geography and using acquired knowledge about the student's educational context to help plan learning experiences. As Lambert (1997) states, the purpose of assessment is perhaps most usefully characterised as a process of 'getting to know' students.

Before considering in more detail the different approaches to assessment we might reflect upon two important points. Firstly, learning objectives within lesson plans and schemes of work are central to assessment. The National Curriculum for Geography is based upon programmes of study for each key stage, from which teachers derive learning objectives and opportunities for assessment. Therefore planning based on the programmes of study should set out clear learning objectives and assessment/performance criteria before any teaching begins.

oto: Margaret Roberts.

Secondly, marking students' work requires careful consideration. It provides an initial point of dialogue between teacher and learner, and the 'rules' of communication have to be understood by the student as well as the teacher if the activity is to prove worthwhile. The actual 'marking' of a piece of work can take a variety of forms, serving different purposes. Some of these purposes are educational and designed to help students to progress, while others may be bureaucratic and used for future summative judgements of student attainment. More information about the mechanics of marking is given in Chapter 4.

Formative and summative assessment

Within key stage 3, GCSE and A/AS-level, assessment serves two purposes: looking forward to help students progress in their day-to-day learning (formative assessment), and looking back to provide information about what they have learned at key points during and at the end of the course (summative assessment).

Formative assessment

This type of assessment helps teachers (and students) monitor and make judgements about their progress. They are broadly 'educational' in purpose. They help us tell both parties what has been learned, what problems there are in the current learning process, and which areas of study may need further work. The purpose of formative assessment is therefore to help diagnose what students do well, and what they struggle with, so that future teaching and learning can more closely match the students' needs. The forms of assessment which help to make such diagnoses are extremely varied and can be either formal or informal – they could be a question and answer session in class, discussion work or written work, class tests or observations of how groups of children work.

Summative assessments

These are made at the end of a unit of work or course, to summarise students' performance. Summative assessments are usually more formal and designed for a different range of purposes. These include informing parents and future teachers about students' attainment, helping teachers evaluate the success of their teaching and, increasingly, judging school effectiveness. They can also be used to grade or level students' attainments. The traditional examination grades awarded for GCSE, A- and AS-levels are, therefore, summative assessments, as are the national curriculum levels awarded at the end of key stage 3. These results are public and can be used for purposes other than educational ones – creating league tables, as entry qualifications for other courses, or in job applications. As such they need to be reliable and standardised. However, this is not a simple process. Much debate has occurred recently about the validity of grades, or levels, awarded by different teacher examiners, awarding bodies, and within different subjects at GCSE, A- and AS-levels.

Summative assessments can also have formative and evaluative elements; for example, they can make an important contribution to target setting. Key stage 3,

GCSE and A/AS-level results are valuable sources of information for analysing 'value added' and for evaluating the effectiveness of teaching in the department, prioritising and setting targets for improvement. The results of termly or other assessments provide opportunities for setting meaningful targets for students and helping them to reach these targets.

Objectivity is almost certainly impossible in any form of assessment. The whole process of assessing children is dependent on the subjective judgements of teachers and examiners, albeit using objective criteria. However, there is still faith in summative assessments being objective and reliable, with A-level especially representing a 'gold standard'. But a gold standard is of no practical use unless we can use the information gained through assessment to inform our decisions about future teaching strategies. This evidence base can be applied to evaluate teaching and learning and subsequently modify, or reinforce, the teaching and learning methods used.

Photo: Margaret Roberts.

Validity and reliability

Validity and reliability are most often issues in formal assessments. They are fundamentally about fairness and equality of opportunity: whether the assessment methods used actually provide information about what we want to assess (validity), and whether these assessments are standardised and would produce the same result if repeated (reliability).

Criteria and norm referencing

Criteria-referenced assessment systems 'fix' the standard of performance by stating criteria (or, in the national curriculum, the Levels) against which students will be assessed. Any student who meets the given criteria is 'awarded' with that Level. Any number of students can therefore 'pass' at different Levels – achievement does not depend upon the performance of others (as is the case in norm referencing). Criteria-referenced assessment is based on acknowledging *positive achievement related to learning objectives.* It is central to formative, as well as summative, assessment for key stage 3 and GCSE.

One of the complications of the criteria-referencing system is the making of judgements about the levels of performance achieved by students. Here the concept of where a student's attainment 'best fits' within a given range of detailed criteria becomes a key professional judgement.

By contrast, in a system of norm-referenced assessment we might test a cohort of students and then ascribe grades to certain sections of this population. For example, the students achieving the top 15 per cent of marks may all be awarded an A grade, whilst the bottom 10 per cent will be ungraded. Here students' work is being judged in comparison with that of other students and there is no fixed standard that has to be achieved to be awarded a particular grade. To use an oversimplified example, if all the students do 'well' on the test and score high marks, the 'bottom' 10 per cent will *still* be ungraded despite their generally pleasing performances! Some of them must inevitably 'fail' in this assessment system.

It appears that criteria referencing is by far the better, and fairer, system of assessment. However, both systems can be applied well or badly, and can serve a range of requirements beyond those of enhancing the quality of education within the classroom. Few assessment systems operate a pure form of either approach; to provide exact, unambiguous criteria of achievement in a subject such as geography is impossible.

'Official' assessment systems

Many teachers have to adhere to what might be loosely termed 'official' assessment systems with respect to summative assessments. These outline, clarify and standardise the means and outcomes of the assessment of students' learning. Lambert describes these 'official' assessment systems as an 'assessment industry' made up of a:

> 'community of experts who, with all their technical knowledge and not inconsiderable resources, have produced what can appear to be a separate yet highly influential culture within `the education world' (Lambert, 1996, p. 260).

In the 1990s the role of teacher assessment was strengthened, partly as a result of the introduction of publicly reported, summative assessment at the end of year 9. As Westaway and Rawling state, the aim of this summative levelling of students at the end of key stage 3 is to make a rounded judgement which:

> • 'is based on knowledge of how the student performs across a range of contexts;
>
> • takes into account strengths and weaknesses of the student's performance
>
> • is checked against adjacent level descriptions to ensure that the level awarded is the closest match to the student's performance' (Westaway and Rawling, 1997, p. 40).

It is important to include a variety of assessment types – from written tasks and tests to oral work, fieldwork, groupwork and information and communications technology (ICT) – in order to ensure good quality teacher assessment which supports student learning across the key stages. This will also provide good evidence of positive achievement in a range of contexts – the most appropriate and valid basis for making professional judgements at the end of key stage 3. However, most 'official' assessment is external and raises questions as to its reliability. For the GCSE, A- and AS-levels, the Qualifications and Curriculum Authority (QCA) has established codes of practice, national criteria and systematic scrutinies which check that awarding bodies conform to standard procedures.

The use of level descriptions in an official assessment system

Level descriptions are central to the summative assessment of student performance at key stage 3. The National Curriculum for Geography has eight level descriptions (and one other for 'exceptional performance') which are made up of brief statements about the aspects of geographical attainment we need to assess: places, patterns and processes, environmental relationships and issues, and enquiry skills. Progression is described as moving from one Level Description to the next, although we would not expect the steps (or incline!) of this progression to be universally agreed upon by geographers (see page 27).

The level description is used as a 'best fit' descriptor, so it is inappropriate to disaggregate each level description completely and use its component parts as a 'tick list' of content or skills to be assessed. Initially, some aspect of dissection is required – to achieve a fuller understanding of what the levels mean in terms of teaching and assessing students. However, this should not create a multitude of 'statements of attainment' to be assessed separately, such a system failed spectacularly in the early 1990s. The publication of the four aspects of performance is an important advance in focusing teachers'

Photo: Margaret Roberts.

professional judgements. The key point is that student attainment in geography, which is a synthesising and integrative subject, is made up of a 'whole' performance in a combination of skills, place knowledge, understanding and geographical themes. If we break up the assessment of this synthesis we lose some of the essence of geographical attainment.

As teachers we must first clarify our own understanding of what the levels mean, how they may be applied and whether different student assessments provide the necessary evidence for making 'best fit' judgements of performance. Reaching agreement about these understandings within a department is an important stage in improving the validity and reliability of a school's judgements. The documents produced by SCAA (1996) and ACAC (1996), *Expectations in Geography at Key Stages 1 and 2* and *Exemplification of Standards: Geography key stage 3* will provide support. Portfolios, either of selected elements of an individual student's work or compiled from a range of students' performances on certain assessment tasks, are an important aid to the levelling process.

Conclusion

Although it is possible to think about assessment in both theoretical and practical ways, and to try to bring both spheres closer together, it is worth reminding ourselves of the fallibility of many assessment methods. Meaningful assessment is notoriously difficult to achieve, since the expectations placed upon its results are often unrealistic or ill founded. Assessment is more an 'art' than a 'science', and the convergence of theory and practice is not always straightforward. Wiegand illustrates this point in the following statement:

> 'Individual teacher assessment can be notoriously unreliable. We are easily misled by the "halo effect" of neatly presented written work or socially skilled children's conversation into thinking that a particular student's understanding is greater than it in fact is. Perhaps we also tend to focus too readily on what children cannot do rather than on what they can. Student performance needs to be gathered from as wide a range of sources as possible' (Wiegand, 1997, p. 267).

The rise of teacher assessment within the national curriculum makes it essential that we as geography teachers discuss our shared understanding of what constitutes student attainment, progression and valid assessment within geography.

Professional development activities

1 **Reviewing assessment methods**
* **Complete a small audit of the different assessment methods used at key stage 3 or key stage 4.**
* **Do you find that one or two methods of assessment dominate in your department?**

2 **Using assessment effectively**
* **What are the uses to which this assessment information is put for any particular year group?**

3 **Developing the role of assessment**
* **If assessment is dominated by one or two methods are there other forms of assessment which should be introduced?**
* **What might these other forms of assessment help you to do in educational and/or bureaucratic terms?**

Photo: Richard Greenhill.

Chapter 3

Planning for progression and assessment

- **How can assessment work to support students' attainment and progress in geography?**
- **How and when should we assess?**

The main issues explored in this chapter are that:

- continuity and progression in the geography curriculum are central to assessment planning;
- the national curriculum level descriptions are useful for helping to set a context for planning work – allowing achievement at a variety of levels;
- as students progress, the geographical work they do should get harder;
- planning for assessment should take place at long-, medium- and short-term;
- a wide range of assessment activities should be planned so that all students have an opportunity to show what they know, understand and can do;

- clear learning objectives are essential to good assessment.

This chapter outlines what we mean by continuity and progression in student's learning and demonstrates how planning for continuity and progression, and planning for assessment, relate to each other and promote achievement. It shows how different assessment strategies and purposes can be matched in the short-, medium- and long-term. The following section (pages 24-28) is based on Bennetts' (1995) discussion of continuity and progression.

What do we mean by continuity and progression?

Continuity is an essential complement to progression. A concern for continuity helps to guide students' progress within and between key stages. The geography Order supports continuity from age 5 to 14 by providing a common framework for planning in the programmes of study and common descriptions of achievement in the level descriptions. The revised 2000 programme of study sets out the common elements of geography which provide continuity of experience across the key stages. Beyond the national curriculum, GCSE criteria have been amended to link with the programme of study. Such common frameworks bring together some general assumptions about the nature of geography education, its content, organisation and types of learning activity.

Continuity can be summarised as:

- **a feature of course design which maps out and links students' experiences;**
- **enabling students to build on previous experiences and learning;**
- **helping students to acquire and develop geographical knowledge, understanding and skills, as well as broader competencies such as information and communications technology, in a structured way.**

Heads of department can support continuity by building a common understanding of geography within their department. The key features of geography are:

- **a focus on place study – where places are, what they are like, how they change and their links with other places;**
- **a concern with relationships between people and environments;**
- **the use of maps and other sources of geographical information;**
- **a focus on geographical enquiry to investigate places, themes and issues.**

Progression describes how students' learning advances. We use it to describe how we plan for these advances, as well as the process itself. We can think of it as an incline, a series of steps or a spiral of knowledge, understanding, skills, attitudes and values (Figure 1). Progression is therefore:

- **related to curriculum design – how the structure helps and promotes advances in learning;**
- **the gains in knowledge, understanding, skills and competencies students actually achieve.**

We can support progression in the longer term by planning to revisit key elements of geography, for example, recurrent themes, key concepts and groups of skills. This is commonly achieved through a spiral approach to curriculum planning. It is also worth remembering that the study of geography contributes to a wide range of more general capabilities such as language, numeracy, reference skills and problem solving.

Teachers are also concerned with supporting progression in the medium and short term:

- **building on what students have already experienced and achieved;**
- **focusing on what they can be expected to do at the time;**
- **matching tasks to capabilities and moving students on to the next stage of learning (e.g. moving from the concrete to more general concepts).**

At long,- medium- and short-term levels, planning for students' progress is closely related to achievements and it is crucial to consider the role of assessment in monitoring students' progress and in matching provision to meet their needs.

Planning for progression and achievement in geography

Planning for progression links two aspects of planning concerned with students' learning: progression in learning objectives, linked with the programmes of study and hence with geography as a subject, and progression in attainment, linked with the level descriptions and broad ideas about expectations and 'standards'. It is useful to have both of these aspects in mind as part of the process of planning; Figure 2 (page 29) the relationship between them at the long-, medium- and short-term levels of planning. Both programmes of study and level descriptions were developed through a 'best practice' model rather than through research about how students learn geography, so each is a starting point for professional judgements, rather than a

(a)

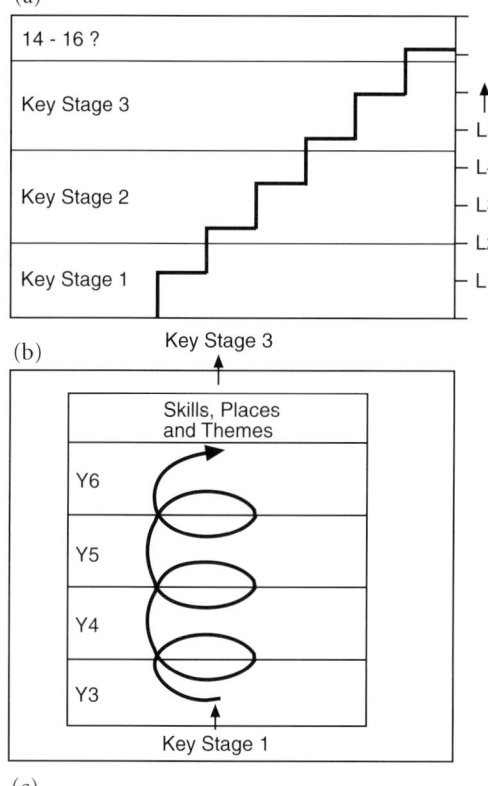

(b)

(c)

(d)

definitive solution to planning learning and assessment opportunities in geography education.

Progression in the programmes of study

The programmes of study for geography help to guide progression and maintain continuity between the key stages, although there is some evidence that the transition from primary to secondary schools often results in a lack of progress or even a regression between key stages 2 and 3 (see QCA, 1998; Jones, 1999). Within key stage 3, planning for progression is often based on our intuitive understanding of which concepts and skills are more or less demanding, because there is no systematic support within the programmes of study. Bennetts (1995) suggests that a focus on the following areas will improve progression:

Photo: Jacky Chapman/Format.

Figure 1: Some models of progression:

(a) over the key stages – (QCA's model) a series of big steps,

(b) across the key stages – a spiral,

(c) within a topic or unit – an incline, and

(d) within a lesson or group of lessons – some small steps or even sudden leaps.

Breadth of geographical knowledge
is related to curriculum content, for
example, where places are. Including
studies of a range of places and themes
over the key stage should support this,
at different and contexts appropriate to
the students' age, e.g. local, UK, EU,
global. Information must be accurate and
relevant to be useful. Planning will need
to identify:

- Which knowledge can be reinforced
  and revisited?
- Which information is intended to be used
  by students as part of the learning
  process; which should be memorised for
  later recall?

Depth of geographical understanding
is linked to the development of
geographical ideas and concepts by
students. Understanding is related to
their ability to describe and explain
patterns, relationships and changes and
later to apply these to new situations in
order to interpret and evaluate.
Planning needs to address:

- linking increasingly complex ideas to
  concrete examples, moving from
  concrete to abstract;
- identifying key ideas and lines of
  progression through themes from
  the programmes of study,
  e.g. weather, settlement.

The development and use of skills,
including enquiry skills (e.g. asking
questions), specific techniques and
capabilities (e.g. directions, maps, ICT)
and broad categories of abilities (e.g.
describing, explaining). Planning needs
to address:

- identifying appropriate contexts for skill
  development, including enquiry skills;
- building a systematic approach to
  developing specific skills across
  the key stage;
- giving students opportunities to improve
  the quality of their understanding and
  application of skills.

Attitudes and values are an important
aspect of developing understanding of a
range of issues in the geography Order.
Progression is linked to students' ability
to discuss, empathise and diagnose
issues, so planning needs to create:

- opportunities for students to develop
  understanding of how peoples' attitudes
  and values influence their actions;
- opportunities to discuss these issues and
  to develop views of their own.

	Planning for progression: learning objectives	Planning for progression: attainment and target setting
Long term	• Learning objectives for the key stage are general and closely related to the programme of study or GCSE syllabus, i.e. knowledge, understanding and skills. • To promote progression over the key stage, decisions focus on how the programme of study/syllabus can be divided into topics or study units, and when these are planned. For example, a spiral approach to the key stage plan helps students revisit, develop and extend their knowledge, concepts and skills.	• The level descriptions in geography are designed as benchmarks against which to assess students' attainment over key stage 3 as a whole. • Level descriptions are useful as a focus for long-term evaluation of how successful the curriculum has been in promoting learning and providing opportunities for students to show their attainments. • This helps to set departmental targets and to make decisions about where to focus next to raise achievement and 'standards'.
Medium term	• Here progression is concerned with the development of knowledge, understanding and skills within a topic or unit. • The focus is on planning sequences of learning objectives that will help support students' progress, e.g. by broadening and deepening their knowledge and understanding, and relating these objectives to assessment. • Evaluation at the end of the unit helps focus on the progress students have made.	• Key decisions focus on identifying assessment opportunities to match the learning objectives. These should be developmental, to match progression over the unit as a whole. • Here the level descriptions are less useful, although they may help in deciding the level of demand of activities and the pitch of assessment. • Student self-assessment and target setting help support their progress towards the next stages in their learning.
Short term	• Progression in individual lessons is concerned with the (often small) steps students make in the development of knowledge, understanding and skills. • Planning is focused on deciding on specific objectives, activities and opportunities for assessment, and on differentiation. • So progression is an integral part of teaching and learning, related to deciding strategies for individuals and groups, assessing and monitoring progress and deciding future objectives.	• Assessment within lessons can be based on a range of informal and more formal strategies, such as observing and talking to students and marking their work. • The focus is on using information gained from these assessments to decide the next step in their learning, in other words supporting progression at the most important level. • Here the level descriptions are of little value, since they relate to the key stage as a whole and the steps between them are large.

Figure 2: Progression in objectives and attainment.

Progression in the level descriptions

There is more support for progression within the level descriptions, based on a general move from knowledge at the lowest levels, through comprehension and analysis, to synthesis and evaluation at the highest. SCAA (1996a) outlines what have become 'strands' through the level descriptions by identifying four aspects of attainment in national curriculum geography; in Curriculum 2000, these have become the framework for organising the programmes of study too.

The curriculum planning process will need to ensure that students are given the opportunity, across the key stage, to achieve at a range of levels. In addition, the assessment opportunities should allow the teacher to build up enough relevant evidence to make the soundest possible judgement at the end of the key stage. The two SCAA exemplification documents: *Expectations in Geography at Key Stages 1 and 2* (1997a) and *Exemplification of Standards – Geography, key stage 3* (1996a), supplemented by the ACAC *Exemplification of Standards – Geography, key stage 3* (1996), can be used to support this process in two ways.

First, the materials can be used to identify general paths for progression for groups of students or for individuals, in relation to the four 'strands'. Second, the material can be used to identify strengths and weaknesses in teaching and learning and, subsequently, targets to focus on to improve students' progress in following years. For example, this type of evaluation might show the need to undertake more enquiry work or to study places on a wider range of scales. On a straightforward level each teacher needs to ensure, for example, that a place study of Brazil in year 9 should explore more difficult concepts than a study of Italy in year 8. There's no reason why Brazil is inherently harder to study than Italy – it is the curriculum planner's job to ensure, in this context, that it is.

Progression in enquiry

QCA (1998) identifies the three aspects of enquiry in the programmes of study which develop across key stages 1 to 3:

- the role of questions as a focus for investigation;
- the use of skills, evidence and resources;
- reasoning, concluding and communicating findings.

Progression in these three aspects is mapped out in Figure 3. QCA argues that progression in enquiry is also partly related to context, that is, what is being investigated (QCA, 1998). Here we can see progression as being characterised by:

- investigations being carried out in the context of places at an **increasing range of scales** (from Level 2);
- an increasing emphasis on **comparison** and on **explanations** (from Level 3);
- an increasing emphasis on **processes** (from Level 4);
- studies which recognise **ways in which places are linked** (from Level 5);
- an increasing emphasis on **change** (from Level 6) and on **interaction between physical and human processes** (from Level 7).

Practical issues – assessment on a daily basis?

Discussions about different approaches to assessment and the types of system currently in use are important. However, they should not draw us away from the essential issues of what we assess and how we assess it. What are we looking for in the classroom when we assess students' work?

Some purposes for assessment

Assessment purposes include:

- to check that work has been fully understood and skills acquired;
- to make judgements about students' progress (what the student knows, understands and can do);
- to measure achievement against a given learning objective;
- to give students feedback on their learning;
- to plan for the next stage of student(s) learning;
- to monitor and evaluate the effectiveness of teaching;
- to give feedback to others about teaching and learning within geography.

Stage of enquiry Level	**Type of performance looked for and referred to in programmes of study:**		
	Paragraph 2a – identify questions, issues and a sequence of investigation	**Paragraph 2b** – identify evidence; collect, record and present it	**Paragraph 2c** – analyse, evaluate, draw conclusions and communicate findings
Level 3	Respond to a range of questions	Use skills and sources of evidence	Offer reasons for observations and judgements
Level 4	Suggest suitable geographical questions for study	Use a range of skills and evidence	Communicate findings using appropriate vocabulary
Level 5	Identify relevant geographical questions	Select and use appropriate skills and evidence	Reach plausible conclusions and present findings both graphically and in writing
Level 6	Identify relevant questions and suggest appropriate sequences of investigation	Select and make use of a wide range of skills and evidence	Present conclusions that are consistent with the evidence
Level 7	With growing independence, identify geographical questions, establish a sequence of investigation	Select and use accurately a wide range of skills and evidence	Begin to reach substantiated conclusions
Level 8	Show independence in identifying appropriate geographical questions and implement an effective sequence of investigation	Select and use effectively and accurately a wide range of skills	Reach substantiated conclusions
Exceptional performance	Undertake geographical enquiries independently	Use accurately a wide range of skills and evidence	Reach substantiated conclusions, presented effectively and accurately. Evaluate work by suggesting improvements in approach and further lines of enquiry

Figure 3: Progression in enquiry.

Some assessments may serve more than one of the purposes stated above, or meet a need not mentioned here. We should be careful when trying to gather multiple pieces of information from one type of assessment, as the validity and reliability of this information tends to become suspect. We need a range of different assessment information and evidence to discover accurately what students know, understand and can do. Some students may perform better in one kind of assessment than another, some may have an 'off day' if assessed just on one 'high stakes' assessment, whilst certain forms of assessment will not access the specific information we may require. With this in mind, it may be worth planning a variety of assessment items which attempt to assess different aspects of students' abilities and attainment (such as, for example, communication skills, recall, decision-making, evaluation and empathy).

One important, but often neglected, component in the assessment system is the student as learner. Does he or she realise the purpose of the assessment? What it means? How to interpret it? How to progress from here? This is important because without the students knowing what the next steps should be in their learning of geography, and beginning to self-assess their progress, the point of assessment may be lost. We should therefore share the objectives with students – let them know what we (think) we know, and help them to assess their own strengths and weaknesses. Pupils should ultimately be able to set their own targets to improve the quality of their learning in geography.

Planning assessment opportunities

The old adage about assessment opportunities being part of the curriculum planning process still holds true. Assessment in geography is not something which concerns only teachers in years 9 and 11 – the years associated with public, summative assessment. Planning for assessment will be part of a whole school/college process and planning for assessment in geography will need to be addressed at each of the following levels:

- **whole school/college;**
- **department key stage plan;**
- **unit of work or topic;**
- **individual lesson.**

The process of planning for assessment and recording within the geography curriculum is summarised in Figure 4.

Long-term assessment planning

Long-term assessment planning is about assessment policy. For example, decisions will have to be made about the type and frequency of assessment opportunities, both formal and informal, across the key stage. Departmental policy will also be governed by the organisation of whole school requirements, such as end-of-year reporting or half-termly grades.

Medium-term assessment planning

The purpose of devising medium-term assessment strategies is to supplement and anchor more informal, everyday judgements, by providing opportunities to assess in greater depth. Organising geographical work in key stage 3 into geographical enquiries can make the assessment task much more straightforward (see Chapter 5). There may also be a role for end-of-unit tasks, for example, those provided by SCAA (1996b), school-designed tests or other 'special assessment occasions'. In planning geographical work in the medium term, teachers will pose the following questions:

- **What will I do?** *The objectives of the topic or unit of work related to the programmes of study.*
- **What will they learn?** *The students will know, understand and be able to ...*
- **What will they do?** *Sequence of activities, tasks, assignments, etc.*
- **How will I provide access?** *By employing differentiation strategies.*
- **How will I know they have learned it?** *Ways of collecting evidence and demonstrated achievement criteria.*

Timescale	Learning objectives ▼ Assessment strategies	Records (supplementing teachers' knowledge)	Purpose
Short term (from week-to-week)	• discussion and observation of students working • questioning • on-going marking	• teachers' notes/log • annotations on student's work • regular marking to agreed policy • in-depth written comments	Diagnostic/formative: • to inform interventions/next steps • to give feedback to students and set short-term targets • to inform future plans • to monitor and make judgements about progress in the short term
Medium term (over a term /topic)	• common assessment tasks/activities • QCA tasks • student self-assessment	• class record • samples of students' work • student awards/credits	Formative/summative: • to give feedback to students and agree targets for improvement related to criteria • to monitor and make judgements about progress
Long term (over a year /key stage)	• using professional judgements to summarise attainment • yearly exams • end of key stage judgement about level (key stage 3) • coursework (GCSE)	• reports • portfolio	Summative/evaluative: • to inform the next teacher • to inform parents • to evaluate, monitor and exemplify standards and attainment • to select, set and monitor departmental targets for improvement

Figure 4: A framework for assessing, recording and reporting geography.

QCA's schemes of work for geography at key stage 3 (QCA, 2000) contain a number of unit plans based on the principles of planning for achievement. They provide a good model for developing individual departments' medium-term plans (Figure 5).

QCA's unit plans also provide useful expectations about students' attainment at the end of the unit, linked with the overall objectives (see Chapter 5).

These medium-term plans are also the bridge towards short-term planning, since each section provides the objectives which are interpreted in more detail in individual lessons.

Short-term assessment planning

Short-term learning objectives, or learning intentions, are relatively easy to use to help define student outcomes. The objectives specify what we want the students to know, understand, or to be able to do as a result of the work we plan. The objectives could be couched as 'key questions', where the teacher is able to use similar key questions for students of different ages and abilities but will change the performance criteria according to the target student 'audience'. Thus the question: 'Where is this place?' could be answered by finding the place in an atlas and giving a page number reference or an alpha-numeric co-ordinate on the page; or a six-figure co-ordinate; or latitude and longitude reference, according to the pre-determined performance criteria. Short-term objectives, whichever style we use, underpin good practice in focused assessment of teaching and learning.

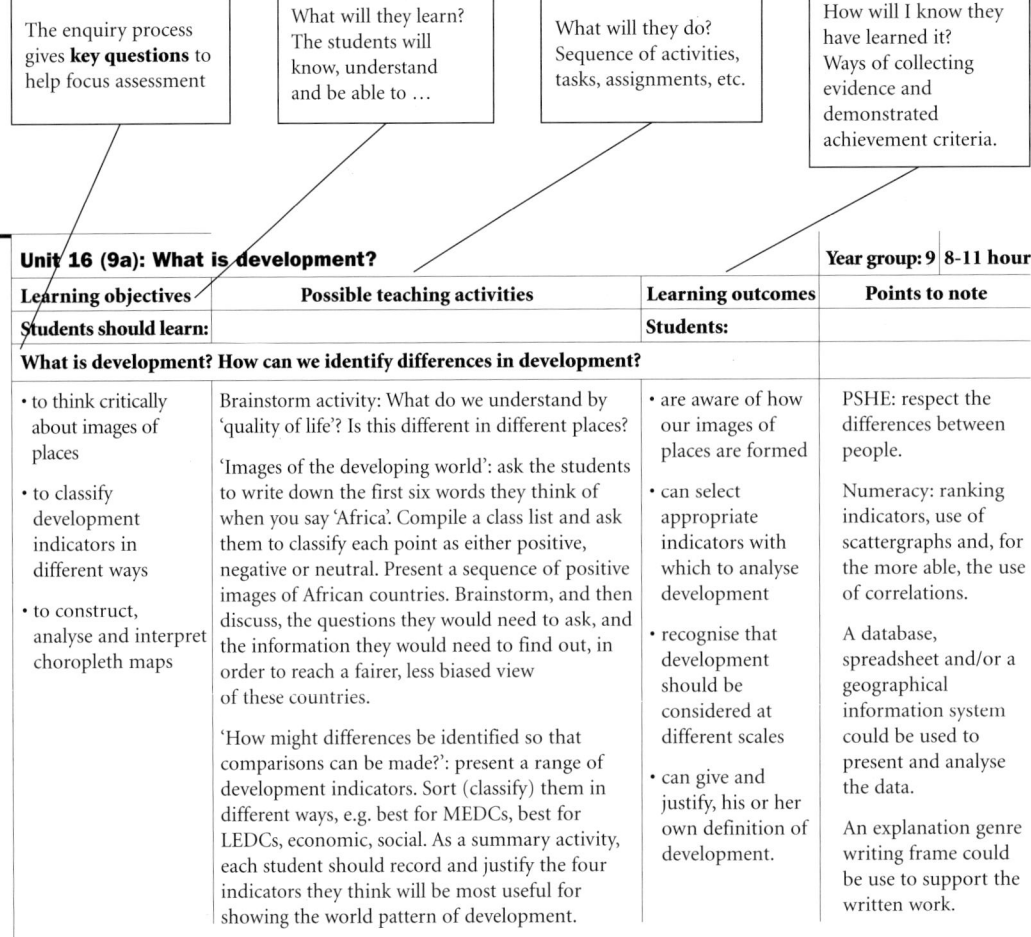

The enquiry process gives **key questions** to help focus assessment

What will they learn? The students will know, understand and be able to …

What will they do? Sequence of activities, tasks, assignments, etc.

How will I know they have learned it? Ways of collecting evidence and demonstrated achievement criteria.

Unit 16 (9a): What is development?   Year group: 9 8-11 hours

Learning objectives	Possible teaching activities	Learning outcomes	Points to note
Students should learn:		Students:	
What is development? How can we identify differences in development?			
• to think critically about images of places • to classify development indicators in different ways • to construct, analyse and interpret choropleth maps	Brainstorm activity: What do we understand by 'quality of life'? Is this different in different places? 'Images of the developing world': ask the students to write down the first six words they think of when you say 'Africa'. Compile a class list and ask them to classify each point as either positive, negative or neutral. Present a sequence of positive images of African countries. Brainstorm, and then discuss, the questions they would need to ask, and the information they would need to find out, in order to reach a fairer, less biased view of these countries. 'How might differences be identified so that comparisons can be made?': present a range of development indicators. Sort (classify) them in different ways, e.g. best for MEDCs, best for LEDCs, economic, social. As a summary activity, each student should record and justify the four indicators they think will be most useful for showing the world pattern of development.	• are aware of how our images of places are formed • can select appropriate indicators with which to analyse development • recognise that development should be considered at different scales • can give and justify, his or her own definition of development.	PSHE: respect the differences between people. Numeracy: ranking indicators, use of scattergraphs and, for the more able, the use of correlations. A database, spreadsheet and/or a geographical information system could be used to present and analyse the data. An explanation genre writing frame could be use to support the written work.

Figure 5: Assessment through medium-term plans. Source: QCA, 2000.

Summary

Planning for assessment opportunities is an integral part of the process of curriculum planning. Progression and continuity are developed using the feedback process of assessment in the long, medium and short term. Assessment is a tool for both teacher and student for judging the pace and extent of progression, but above all ensuring that progression takes place. Students must be assessed by as wide a variety of methods as possible to allow them to succeed in different contexts – by this method, assessment can and should be fun. The next three chapters focus on the 'how' of assessment in the short, medium and longer terms.

Professional development activities

1. Planning learning to include assessment

Planning should integrate the curriculum, teaching materials and learning styles with assessment opportunities and outcomes. Ask yourself which of these questions can be applied to your lesson, the unit of work, or departmental policy:

- What are the students' needs?
- What have the students and I identified as learning objectives/targets?
- What should the students learn?
- What sort of responses might students give? Am I prepared for a variety of comments?
- How will I identify and respond to evidence of achievement?
- How are students able to recognise their achievements?
- How will we maintain a record?

2. Reviewing assessment strategy and purposes

Photocopy Figure 4 and use it as a focus for departmental discussion, for example:

- Which strategies are part of your assessment and recording practice?
- Are there any additional strategies you need to consider?
- Do you agree with the purposes of assessment at each level?

3. Reviewing progression

Collect examples of students' work on a common theme, e.g. places, from years 7, 9 and 11.

- Does the work show appropriate levels of achievement?
- Can you see a clear progression?

Photo: Roger Carter.

Photo: Margaret Roberts, Department of
Educational Studies, University of Sheffield.

Chapter 4

Day-to-day assessment

- **What does formative assessment mean in the classroom context?**
- **How can formative assessment and marking be improved?**

The main issues explored in this chapter are that:

- formative assessment and marking in improving teaching and learning is important;
- teachers use a wide range of strategies in formative assessment;
- formative assessment can be improved through attention to classroom practice;
- clear and consistent marking policies are important means of helping students make progress.

Introduction

Much of the most valuable information about students' achievements comes from day-to-day observation, questioning and discussion as they work. This form of assessment is mainly informal and intuitive, but it has the potential to make most impact on students' progress. It helps to answer the question 'What next?', and is, therefore, at the heart of formative assessment:

> 'assessment ... undertaken by teachers, and by their students in assessing themselves, which provides information to be used as feedback to modify teaching and learning activities in which they are engaged. Such assessment becomes formative assessment when the evidence is actually used to adapt teaching work to meet the needs' (Black and Wiliam, 1998, p. 2).

The information gained from everyday classroom interactions is supplemented by day-to-day recording – most commonly through marking students' work – and makes an important contribution to later professional judgements (see Chapters 5 and 6). It is important to emphasise that although marking can make a significant contribution to formative assessment (especially through the use of extended comments and short-term targets), formative assessment is not synonymous with marking. The next section explains the role of formative assessment in more depth.

Formative assessment

Formative assessment is central to teaching and learning. It helps us to understand and make judgements about what students know, understand and can do, what are their strengths, weaknesses and any misconceptions, and what the next steps in their learning should be if they are to make progress. Teachers' formative assessment strategies for individuals, groups or the whole class include:

Informal, formative assessment – mostly in my head

Objectives

- Knowledge/understanding: concept of population density; some regions of the world have high/low population density; relationship with positive/negative features
- Skills: interpret photographs
- Key skills: oracy, paired writing

Being clear about the objectives helps me make informal judgements

Organisation, timing	Focus/activities	Grouping
Introduction 5 minutes	Q/A: recap key terms: population, positive/negative reasons for living in places. Taking through objectives for lesson.	Whole class
10 minutes	• Sort large photographs: one student for high, medium and low density areas. Add some difficult ones. Add large labels. • Model photograph interpretation.	Whole class
20 minutes	• Students: annotate photographs, decide on population density.	Pairs
	• Review: feedback from some pairs. Introduce checklist of positive/negative reasons	Whole class
15 minutes	• Students use checklist to decide positive/negative reasons for density, attempt to locate from country checklist.	Pairs
5 minutes	• Begin process of locating on world map.	
Review 5 minutes	Review reasons for density – examples from class.	Whole class

What do they know/remember? What do I need to emphasise or introduce?

Who needs help with the task or vocabulary?

Any mistakes or misconceptions, or special responses?

Have we met the objectives? What have the students learned?

Differentiation: resource/support/task	**Evaluation** Photo prompts and interpretation worked well, but need to rethink locational info: will start with this next session. Need to reinforce point about countries having areas of different density.	
Some students	**Most students**	**With the exception of**
Shamila and Sabia, Adib: good photo interpretation – detailed/incisive comments. Azlam, Irtham: good oral contributions based on photograph work.	Responded well to photographs and annotation task, and understand density concept. Some reasons for density suggested.	Adman, Zamir made some contribution but didn't quite get the density idea.

I can use this jotter to summarise attainment briefly and work out the next steps

Intervention: quality of annotations poor

Intervention: listening skills

Last bit took longer than I thought: pick up next lesson

Figure 1: Short-term planning: population density lesson (year 8, bottom set).

Figure 2: Short term planning example 2: Italy, north and south (year 9). The lesson follows an original idea by Lucy Kirkham.

Informal, formative assessment: mostly in my head

Objectives
- Knowledge/understanding: review of main differences between N/S Italy; review of key geographical vocabulary
- Skills: interpret/find data from atlas
- Key skills: oracy, reading

Being clear about the objectives helps me make informal judgements

Organisation, timing	Focus/activities	Grouping
Introduction 10 minutes	Recap North/South Italy – Q/A using picture prompts Objectives for session	Whole class
10 minutes	• Letter from young people in Milan/Aliano: What are the main differences? What do we mean by regional differences? Introduce task.	Two students (whole class)
15 minutes	• Students sort cards into north/south features; check/retrieve information from atlas. Once sorted, categorise (climate, soil, etc.) and write into large matrix.	Pairs
10 minutes	• Whole class checks: any difficult terms/cards/categories? • Review – around the class – accuracy, correct any problem areas.	Whole class
15 minutes	• Next task: students write notes into small table (physical geography, economic geography, standards of living). Model on board, then use of connecting words to make paragraphs.	Whole class then individual
Review 5 minutes	Key points from above, then homework: compare regions from notes in paragraph.	Whole class

What do they know/remember? What do I need to emphasise or introduce?

Who needs help (i) with the task? (ii) with any concepts or vocabulary?

Any mistakes, misconceptions or special responses?

Do students understand the method/purpose?

Have we met the objectives? What have students learned?

Differentiation: resource/support Extension task not used	**Evaluation** Letter prompts and cards worked well; next time, direct students to textbook as well as atlas. Next time, need to pick up use of connecting words to build paras and move onto explanations/links.

Marking will help me check progress, give feedback next lesson and provide a record

Some students	Most students	With exception of
Daniel B, Siabhan, Emma, Madeline, Omar, James A, Joseph, Fang Chen: fast and accurate work – good use of notes.	Good knowledge/ understanding of main features and key vocabulary. Good co-operation/group work; willing feedback.	Amardeep, Daniel A. uncertain of some key terms. Need to watch they understand the next task.

I can use this jotter to briefly summarise attainment and work out the next steps

- watching and listening to students as they work;
- questioning, discussing or reviewing work with students;
- marking students' work, perhaps alongside them;
- students reflecting on and assessing their own work;
- agreeing 'what next' with students, that is, short-term targets to improve their work.

To be effective, these strategies need to be based on teacher knowledge and understanding of the learning objectives and of progression in geography (see Chapter 3). Figures 1 and 2 show some strategies in action in two examples of key stage 3 lessons.

There is no mystique about formative assessment – as the Ofsted framework (Ofsted 1995, 1998) makes clear, formative assessment is an essential part of good teaching (Figure 3). It can be improved by focusing on key features of good teaching and learning, for example, sharing objectives and criteria with students and reviewing progress at the end of a session.

We might wish to involve students more closely in formative assessment, for example by:

- **establishing what they already know about a topic at the start of a unit (e.g. by discussing ideas or by concept mapping). This can also be used to review progress, especially at the end of a unit;**
- **marking students' work with them;**
- **marking or commenting on their own or others' work;**
- **more summatively, students could also select their best work at the end of a geography unit, perhaps to add to a portfolio or record of achievement.**

Formative assessment is quite distinct from the department's arrangements for assessment in line with national curriculum requirements, although of course the information gained from day-to-day interaction with students forms a key part of the professional judgements needed to make end-of-key-stage judgements about levels. To set students meaningful targets for improving their work we need to know about their attainment and progress. We can only obtain this information through formative assessment, supplemented by more summative judgements made through 'special assessment occasions' (see Chapter 5).

Do teachers assess students' work thoroughly and constructively, and use assessments to inform teaching?

• Interventions with students, including the marking of work, are used to help students to understand what they need to do to improve their work and make progress.

Clues to the effectiveness of formative assessment are how well teachers listen and respond to students, encourage and, where appropriate, praise them, recognise and handle their misconceptions, build on their responses and steer them towards new learning or clearer understanding. Interactions of this kind play an important part in the support and encouragement of students and may be seen in a variety of contexts including whole class lessons, group work and individual tasks.

Are there effective systems for assessing students' attainment?

Is assessment information used to inform curriculum planning?

• Inspectors should evaluate whether assessments are accurate and used to plan future work and to help students to make progress … Particular attention needs to be given to the use of assessment data in planning a response to the needs of individual students – for example, in modifying teaching programmes for students with special educational needs.

There is a strong link between good teaching and good formative assessment, when teachers use assessment information to help plan the next steps in the work. In successful lessons the teachers use a range of assessment techniques such as well phrased questions, listening to and observing students, and discussing and evaluating the students' written work. These methods provide students with good quality feedback about their work and teachers gain useful knowledge of students' attainment.

Figure 3: What does the Ofsted inspection framework say about formative assessment?
Source: Ofsted, 1995, pp. 74, 78, 84, 1998.

In planning documentation, annotations indicating:

• a change of pace;
• additions, supplementary/extension work;
• work planned but not covered;
• evaluative comments, aspects needing development: where next?

In the classroom

• intervention in students' learning to provide 'on the spot' teaching;
• feedback to individuals, groups, or the whole class, about aspects needing attention;
• target setting for individuals, groups;
• use of open/probing questions;
• provision of extension activities;
• variety of approaches to differentiation providing access to activities;
• students actively involved in the assessment process.

In students' books and on their work, marking which:

• gives students explicit feedback;
• provides explicit teaching, guidance;
• encourages students to reflect on their own achievement;
• results in improvement in subsequent work.

Figure 4: Signs that assessment is being used formatively.
Source: Assessment Team, Birmingham Advisory and Support Service.

Although much formative assessment is day-to-day (or minute-to-minute), informal and intuitive, it does not happen of its own accord; rather it is based on careful planning. So evidence of formative assessment may be found in planning documents, in the lesson itself, and in students' work (Figure 4). Key points to ensure useful and successful formative assessment include:

- **planning takes account of assessment, for example by attention to learning objectives and by targeting groups of students and individuals;**
- **objectives are clear to teachers and students and progress is regularly reviewed;**
- **information about students' achievements feeds into the short-term planning process, for example, to identify students needing additional help;**
- **teachers provide feedback on work completed, progress and next steps.**

One problem with formative assessment is that in England and Wales virtually all recent education policies have promoted formal, external, 'high stakes' assessments, rather than supporting teachers in making and improving their formative assessments. Black and Wiliam argue that there is considerable evidence that more careful attention to formative assessment would lead to 'significant and substantial learning gains' for all ages and especially for lower attainers (Black and Wiliam, 1998, p. 3). These gains would translate into improvements of the equivalent of between one and two grades at GCSE.

Black and Wiliam (1998) also offer advice on classroom practice which will not support formative assessment. Strategies to avoid include:

- **too much generous, unfocused praise;**
- **not sharing approaches with colleagues;**
- **tests, which encourage superficial learning;**
- **an over-emphasis on quantity and presentation;**

• Feedback to any student should be about the particular qualities of his or her work, with advice on what he or she can do to improve, and should avoid comparisons with other students. *For example, by giving students a clear idea about any problems with their work and achievable targets for putting them right.*

• For formative assessment to be productive, students should be trained in self-assessment so that they can understand the main purposes of their learning and thereby grasp what they need to do to achieve. *For example, by giving students feedback on the desired learning goal, their present position, and ways to close the gap.*

• Opportunities for students to express their understanding should be designed into any piece of teaching, for this will initiate the interaction whereby formative assessment aids learning. *For example, by careful attention at the planning stage to learning objectives and activities enabling students to demonstrate positive achievement.*

• The dialogue between students and teachers should be thoughtful, reflective, focused to evoke and explore understanding, and conducted so that all students have an opportunity to think and to express their ideas. *For example, by careful attention to open-ended questioning, and providing opportunities for students to respond to questions individually, in pairs or in groups.*

• Tests and homework exercises can be an invaluable guide to learning, but the exercises must be clear and relevant to learning aims. The feedback on them should give each student guidance on how to improve, and each must be given opportunity and help to work at the improvement. *For example, more frequent short tests linked to objectives are better than infrequent and longer ones with no opportunities for feedback.*

Improved formative assessment is linked with other features, including:

• improved feedback between students and teachers, itself involving changes in classroom practice;

• assumptions about what makes for effective learning, especially the active involvement of learners;

• improving the teaching and learning;

• the effects of assessment on learners' motivation and self-esteem;

• the benefits of involving students in self-assessment.

Figure 5: How to improve formative assessment
After Black and Wiliam, 1998.

• **an overemphasis on marks and grades, rather than personal improvement; this has a particular impact on low attainers;**

• **offering feedback which is 'social' and 'managerial' rather than focused on learning.**

Figure 5 summarises Black and Wiliam's findings about strategies for improving formative assessment.

Marking students' work

Giving careful attention to marking students' work is a key aspect of improving formative assessment (Figure 6). A departmental marking policy which is followed by all teachers and clear to students and parents, will ensure consistency, involve students in the assessment process and help raise standards. It is also an essential part of any system of recording and reporting:

'Scrutiny of students' books and discussion with students provide evidence of the quality of marking, how thoroughly problems are diagnosed, whether comments both encourage and challenge and whether the approaches to marking are consistent. It will be evident in written work whether feedback is having a positive effect' (Ofsted, 1995, p. 75).

Good practice in marking

Good practice in marking should aim to establish a dialogue between teacher and learner. Marking should evaluate students' work using clear criteria which are consistently applied, and should focus on progress as well as achievements in order to support future learning. Key questions are:

• **How are the good features of a piece of work identified?**

• **How do students know what to do to improve their work?**

| A grade – preferably tied to criteria | | Some qualities |

C. *You've described carefully how you carried out your investigation. I like the way you presented what you found out –*
good use of divided bar graphs to show the changes. Next time, try to explain the reasons for your findings; why do you
think the changes happened? You also need to write a proper conclusion to summarise all your main points.

| Targets for improvement |

Figure 6: Detailed comments.

An important decision concerns the tension between how manageable and how useful a marking system is. Students are likely to get most benefit from very detailed comments on every piece of work, but this may not be manageable for the teacher. The department therefore needs to decide the frequency and detail of written comments and their relationship with grades or marks. We might consider, as part of a marking policy:

- **establishing common systems of grading children's work linked to a shared understanding of the grades (an example is shown in Figure 7);**
- **developing criteria for assessment as part of the planning process, sharing the objectives and success criteria with the students;**
- **planning opportunities to make periodic, in-depth assessments, perhaps linked with special assessment occasions (see Chapter 5) or through focused marking with a sample of students, e.g. ten, per week.**

Figure 7 shows some of the tensions behind any system, such as whether to reward effort or achievement (or both), what to do about unfinished or missed work, and whether to use the same criteria across a broad range of ability: is the marking for attainment, or achievement in relation to capability?

Grade	Achievement
A	Very good. You have understood the work in full and explained your ideas in detail.
B	Good. You have understood most of the main points – try to explain your ideas in detail next time.
C	Average. You have understood some of the main points; try to include some detail or a summary next time.
D	Below average. You need to complete more work on this topic.
E	You have handed in little or no work.

Grade	Effort
1	You have tried your hardest: well done.
2	Good: you have worked well on this topic.
3	Quite good, but you usually put more into your work.
4	You need to try harder: this is not your best work.
5	You have put very little effort into this work.

Figure 7: Marking to criteria.

An alternative system is featured in Figure 8. Here the criteria are clearly focused on improvement in relation to key assessment occasions, using the language of the level descriptions to indicate the next stages for students.

Another system which uses arrows to help define progress and share the judgement with students is shown in Figure 9. This system has the advantage that the arrows can be used in a number of ways:

- **to measure progress against the student's last piece of work;**
- **to measure progress against 'safe prediction' and 'challenging target' grades or levels as part of a target setting programme;**
- **to accredit effort, however defined.**

Marking principles and policy

The principles behind a marking policy might include:

- **a focus on positive achievement, and comments which reflect this;**
- **comments which are clear and legible;**
- **a focus on improvement, e.g. aspects of strength/weakness, individual targets;**
- **a system which is manageable and useful, systematic and consistent, transparent and understandable;**
- **a relationship with reality and with general 'standards';**
- **marking which relates to the rest of your assessment system;**
- **a role for the students in the process;**
- **informing parents.**

The geography department's marking policy should be part of the assessment policy (Chapter 8) and fit in with whole-school policy, although there may be tensions with other departments' views on marking. There will also be tensions between the various marking purposes at different times, for example, whether marking is to measure or judge achievement, to challenge students, to encourage them, to focus on improvement targets, or to focus

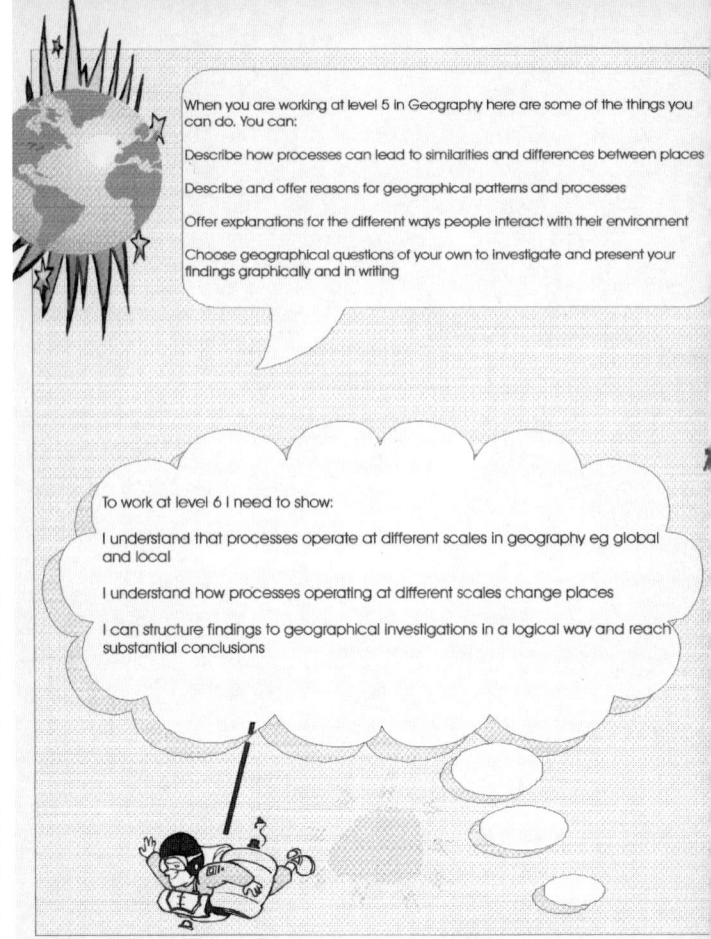

Figure 8: Improving your level in geography. Source: Shenley Court School, Birmingham.

on errors, such as spelling and punctuation, or subject-specific skills and content, or 'work habits' and presentation. At different times, markers might adopt some of the following roles and purposes:

Monitor: Checking that the work has been done
Editor: Helping to rewrite, redraft or improve the next piece of writing/learning
Proof-reader: Correcting errors and trying to ensure they are not repeated next time
Examiner: Grading or levelling work
Teacher: Giving feedback and suggesting improvements, future targets for next time.

There may also be tensions between different methods of grading, for example, for achievement or effort, and whether to use letters or numbers – or even whether to use grades at all; Black and Wiliam (1998) argue they have little impact on *improvement*.

	Used to measure progress since the last piece of work	To measure progress against 'safe prediction' and 'challenging target' grades or levels set as part of a target setting programme	To accredit effort
⬆	This work shows me that you have made good progress in knowledge, skills and understanding since the last piece of work	This work shows me that you are making progress towards your 'challenging target' grade or level	You have made a good effort or you have made a better effort than last time
➡	This work shows me that you have made a little progress in knowledge, skills and understanding since the last piece of work	This work shows me that you are making progress towards your 'safe prediction' grade or level	You have made a satisfactory effort
⬇	This work shows me that you have made no progress in knowledge, skills and understanding since the last piece of work	This work shows me that you are in danger of falling below your 'safe prediction' grade or level	You have made a disappointing effort or You have made less effort than last time

Figure 9: Using arrows as a measure of progress.

Summary: what next?

Many departments already have an effective system of marking. The following checklist may help in reviewing existing marking policies, or designing new ones:

• Agree principles: what do we mean by assessment?

• Agree purposes: why do we mark students' work?

• Agree approaches: What do we focus on? What detail, frequency and tone should written comments have? What is the approach to correcting work, e.g. spelling? What is the role of students?

• Agree a system for implementation, monitoring and evaluation.

Professional development activities

1. Think of a good lesson you have taught in the last two weeks and describe the lesson's objectives and activities to a colleague. Use Figure 4 to identify signs of formative assessment which a visitor to your classroom would have noticed.

2. Study Figure 5, which of the suggested strategies do you use already? Which others could you focus on to improve formative assessment?

3. Self-review on formative assessment; ask yourself the following questions:

• Do I know enough about my students' understanding to be able to help each one of them?

• What are my underlying beliefs about learning and ability? For example: knowledge transmission, coverage, 'delivery' or questioning, thinking, interaction, construction; fixed, inherited IQ; or un-tapped potential

• How do I need to change students' attitudes?

• How does my classroom practice encourage student/teacher interaction?

• How does my classroom practice promote the growth of students' confidence and self-understanding?

Photo: Graham Butt, Department of Education,
University of Birmingham.

Chapter 5

Medium-term assessment: student enquiries

- **What assessments are needed to supplement formative, day-to-day assessments?**
- **How are they best organised?**

The main issues explored within this chapter are that:

- **occasional, in-depth assessments are needed to make more formal judgements about students' progress;**
- **a variety of contexts and forms of assessment support positive achievement;**
- **a focus on student enquiry supports attainment and progression;**
- **well-organised and carefully focused 'special' assessments provide important contributions to the departmental portfolio and a way into level judgements.**

Introduction

Day-to-day, formative assessment arguably gives teachers the most valuable information about students' attainments and has the most impact on their progress (see Chapter 4). However, it is important that these day-to-day judgements are supplemented and anchored by more in-depth, but occasional, assessments to monitor and make judgements about progress in the medium term. It makes sense to focus in-depth assessments on the enquiry process because this aspect of the Order underpins attainment, as QCA point out:

'Geographical enquiry is an integral part of the geography national curriculum requiring students at key stages 1, 2 and 3 to be given opportunities to ask geographical questions and investigate places and themes. The programmes of study at all three key stages refer to opportunities to develop the skills of geographical enquiry and these also form an integral part of the level descriptions' (QCA, 1998, Introduction).

Special assessments

These 'special assessment occasions' may take a variety of forms, such as particular sets of activities or enquiries, the SCAA key stage 3 *Optional Tests and Tasks* (SCAA, 1996b), or short, end-of-unit tests. It is good practice to integrate these occasions with the rest of the term's work, to base them on work the students are likely to enjoy, and to plan a variety of contexts and formats over the key stage. This will help ensure that students with different strengths have opportunities to show positive achievement. What makes these assessments special is that they are likely to be more formal, in the sense that they are identified by teachers and students as being important, with clear objectives, agreed criteria and expectations. It is also good practice to plan these activities or tasks in common across the department, to agree about objectives, shared expectations and to provide judgements about attainment, and comparison of students' performance from different classes.

These medium-term assessments are usefully organised during, or near the end of, a term or unit of work so that their purpose is partly formative. They provide students with feedback about strengths, weaknesses and targets for improvement and an opportunity to include their own self-assessments. Medium-term assessments are also partly summative, contributing to the teacher's general picture of students' attainments which will be reported to parents and used at the end of the key stage. A well-organised system of medium-term assessments provides a useful focus for setting students concrete targets for improvement, makes an important contribution to the recording system, and makes the task of organising a departmental portfolio more straightforward. The Ofsted inspection framework notes that:

'Evidence includes comparison of students' work with teachers' assessments and records. Teachers do not need to keep detailed records to support the assessments they make of each student: they need only collect samples of work which exemplify attainment at each level.
Inspectors should use these samples to examine the comparability of individual teachers' judgements ... Schools must keep formal educational records on every student, including material on academic achievements, other skills and abilities and progress in school, and must update these records at least once a year' (Ofsted, 1995, p. 84).

If these more summative assessments are integrated with other activities across a unit of work, it makes sense that they should be highlighted in some way on the medium-term or unit plans. The schemes of work for key stage 3 (QCA, 2000) show two ways of approaching this. One method is to highlight key aspects of enquiry on the plans, as described above, as a focus for in-depth assessment. Another is to use the 'Expectations' section of a unit; this shows what the expected learning outcomes of the unit of work are for most students, for students who have made less progress, and for students who have made more progress, in relation to the objectives of the unit. These differentiated outcomes have a flavour of aspects of the relevant level descriptions, providing both a summary of attainment over the unit and an agenda for future learning. Although assessment in relation to these expected outcomes is likely to be based on teachers' formative judgements over the course of the work, they provide a useful focus for a more summative task or other special assessment occasion.

The information from these assessments can also be valuable in reviewing the department's plans, for example:

- **At the end of each term or half-term, have the learning objectives specified in the unit of work been covered?**
- **To what extent have students met the learning objectives?**
- **How many learning objectives are manageable in the time?**
- **How is students' attainment of those objectives assessed, and what information best supports the assessment?**
- **Do the learning objectives reflect the range of student's abilities?**
- **Do they stretch the most and least able appropriately? To what extent have these students been able to demonstrate progress and positive achievement? (Adapted from: SCAA, 1997b, p. 5.)**

Using *Exemplification of Standards* to identify progression

There has been some debate nationally about whether level descriptions should or could be applied to individual pieces of work. The debate has been fuelled by the students' need for an indication of the levels of their achievement on individual pieces of work; it is also important that teachers in general can monitor their students' progress and start to 'get their heads round' levels long before they are required to report them to parents.

Exemplification of Standards (SCAA, 1996a) goes some way towards resolving the debate by clarifying progression and expectations in the geography Order. It identifies four aspects of performance (places, patterns and processes, environmental relationships and issues, and enquiry and skills) among the level descriptions which help describe how students progress in their geographical knowledge, understanding and skills. *Exemplification of Standards* recognises that an example of a student's work will show performance in different aspects, but not necessarily all aspects.

Medium-term assessment in practice: case study

The following example of structured student enquiries exemplifies an assessment process which has been applied by teachers working in John Kyrle High School, a maintained, co-educational comprehensive school with 160 to 190 students in each year of key stage 3. The geography department chose to place student investigations at the heart of the assessment process at key stage 3. Each student builds up a portfolio containing up to ten of her or his assessed investigations – and other assessed pieces of work (see Chapter 6). This ensures that students have the opportunity to gain essential enquiry skills. The approach also helped the department to move away from an over-reliance on teacher/textbook-directed activities.

The assessment of the student investigations is a formative process: each student plans her or his investigation and completes a simple form to which the teacher adds comments before the student goes any further. After the teacher has assessed a piece of work, each student completes a self-evaluation. At the end of year 9, teachers will review the assessed work in each student's portfolio to make a summative judgement about which level description best fits that student's overall performance (see Section 2 and chapter on levelling in SCAA, 1996a). The summative judgement will be informed by the formative assessments with which the teacher has been monitoring each student's progress.

The need for a straightforward assessment model prompted the department to produce a base, A4-sized 'grid' to characterise the full range of student performance at different levels (Figure 1). This grid is a first reference point during the planning of appropriate assessment opportunities. The grid may also be adapted to create a criterion-referenced marking sheet against which an individual student's work on a specific investigation may be assessed. When each assessed piece of work is returned, a student may be told that it contains characteristics of particular levels of performance, but students are discouraged from thinking that they have fully achieved any particular level until the end of the key stage.

Theme	Foundation (Levels 1-3)	Intermediate (Levels 4-6) *A range of places and themes at more than one scale*	Advanced (Levels 7- Exceptional performance) *A wide range of places and themes at various scales*
Places	Identifying and beginning to offer observations about simple recognisable features of places. Making simple comparisons between individual features of different places.	Becoming aware of how physical and human processes interact to produce distinctive characteristics and that people have different views about these. Drawing out similarities and differences in the character of places and recognising the links between places.	Appreciating how change in physical and/or human processes may be reflected in the changing character and distinctiveness of places and how different viewpoints may influence decisions. Explaining why places are similar or different and evaluating how this affects their character, their future development and their interdependence with other places.
Patterns and processes	Making simple observations about features and patterns in ther environment. Recognising and making observations about simple physical and human processes.	Describing and explaining patterns and relating these to the character of places and environments at different scales. Identifying, describing and explaining physical and human processes and their impact on places and environments.	Making connections between locations, distributions and patterns of features, and understanding how and why these change and with what impacts on people and places. Understanding how interactions between physical and human processes at different scales can influence the character and development of places and environment.
Environmental relationships and issues	Expressing mainly personal and subjective views abut the environment. Identifying and describing easily recognisable examples of the interactions between people and the environment and of attempts to manage these.	Appreciating and finding evidence in a more objective way for the different views and opinions held by others, and recognising these as processes of change. Describing and offering explanations for different examples of environmental change with varied management responses.	Understanding the significance of different viewpoints in influencing environmental policy and decisions. Explaining the origins and character of complex issues and evaluating the impact of management strategies.
Geographical enquiry skills	Drawing on limited experiences and resources to answer simple geographical questions using basic vocabulary. Using simple techniques and undertaking straightforward tasks demonstrated by the teacher.	Drawing on their experience to identify geographical questions, following a structured sequence of investigation and presenting a consistent geographical argument. Becoming aware of and selecting from a range of appropriate techniques, and demonstrating competence in using a wide range of geographical skills and vocabulary.	Demonstrating independence in posing appropriate questions, planning investigations and providing articulate and substantiated arguments. Demonstrating confidence in selecting skills and strategies appropriate to the task, and applying them effectively.

Figure 1: Characterising a student's performance at different levels. Adapted from: SCAA, 1996.

For the information of students in key stage 3 and their teachers

Aim

State the hypothesis you are testing or the questions you are seeking to answer.

Method

Clearly describe how you collected your data and/or evidence. Diagrams are always helpful.

Results

Clearly present your data and/or evidence (neat tables, maps, graphs, photographs, etc.).

Analysis

Describe the major points of your results in words – draw attention to any significant patterns which you notice. You should then attempt to explain the patterns.

Conclusions

Explain what your results mean with reference back to original aims.

Evaluation

Criticisms of method/data/evidence. Suggestions for improvement in future work.

Figure 2: Information on standard layout for a student investigation.

Helen's progress in key stage 3 – year 8

At the start of year 8, students study physical geography. Helen's class carried out an investigation into the rate at which water soaks into various surfaces. The home-made equipment and method were clearly described in class and the students carried out the experiment at home, sometimes working in pairs. A range of different results determined by the students for each surface was collated and tabulated by the teacher for students to note. The students wrote about their experiment (and the group results) as an investigation (their second in key stage 3). The framework for writing about an empirical investigation is given to all students (Figure 2).

This investigation is not open-ended and is largely teacher-directed. This, coupled with the fact that the students have only just embarked on year 8, means that there is little opportunity for a student to perform above Level 6. A criterion-referenced marking sheet for the investigation is shown in Figure 3. Note that the mark sheet does not identify any assessment criteria within the 'places' or 'environmental relationships and issues' aspects.

Helen's work is shown in Figure 4, together with her teacher's comments. Helen's teacher felt that her performance fitted into the lower end of the 'intermediate' category, because she had correctly followed the experimental method and had attempted a conclusion, but had not drawn on her graphical skills to present the data. In terms of patterns and processes, she began to comment on the variations in infiltration rates, but she didn't take this comment far.

Theme	Foundation (Levels 1-3)	Intermediate (Levels 4-6) *A range of places and themes at more than one scale*
Patterns and processes	Observe patterns in the different infiltration rates. Recognise and makes observations about simple physical and human processes influencing infiltration rates.	Shows an awareness of how site conditions may vary due to physical factors (e.g. texture of material) or human factors (e.g. dug soil/compacted soil).
Geographical enquiry skills	Drawing on limited experiences and resources to answer simple geographical questions using basic vocabulary. Using simple techniques and undertaking straightforward tasks demonstrated by the teacher.	Follows a structured sequence of investigation and presents a consistent geographical argument. Selects appropriate data presentation techniques (table and bar graph), and demonstrates competence in applying experimental technique and specialist vocabulary.

Figure 3: Infiltration rate investigation assessment grid. Adapted from: SCAA, 1996.

Hypothesis: grass,   increasing
soil,   infiltration
sand,   rate

Aim: The aim is to measure infiltration rates and test the hypothesis.

Method: We got a plastic tube and pit it 5cm into the grass, then Gemma put a ruler down the middle of it. I poured the water into the tube and when it reached the 15cm mark Gemma started the stopwatch. When it had gone down 5cm she stopped it. We did this for bare soil and sand.

Diagram ?

My results: grass—it took 8 minutes to soak in 5cm.
sand—it took 45 seconds to soak in 5cm.
soil— it took 30 seconds to soak in 5cm.

Class results: cm/min-infiltration rate
sand-0.7-30(0.7-6.7)
grass-0.6-7
soil-0.2-10(1-2)

Better to show this with a graph of some kind (as well as a table) ✓

Analysis: With sand we got 0.7 per minute to 30cm per minute but more poeple got between 0.7 and 6.7cm per minute. There was such a big difference in the numbers because some people used wet sand and others used dry sand and also there are many different kinds. With grass we got between 0.6 and 7 because some of it was wet and some of it was dry.
With soil we got between 0.2 and 10 there is a bit difference because you can get quite a few different types also some peoples gardens might just have been dug.

Conclusion: My hypothesis was right. I know this because I found the middle number in each of the results for grass, soil, sand. The grass's middle number is 3.2 the soil's middle number is 4.9 and the sands middle number is 14.65, so
grass 3.2cm increasing
soil 4.9cm infiltration
sand 14.65cm rate

need to suggest reasons for these differences

Evaluation: Our experiment was quite good but it wasn't very exact. Some of us might have done the experiment on Saturday and the others on Sunday so it was different conditions. (different in what way?) Also we should have done it on wet says, dry days and with wet soil, dry soil, wet sand and dry sand and wet grass and dry grass. Another thing is we should have tried different kinds of sand.

4/5
Corectly follows experimental method.
No graph to present results.
Comment on variations in infiltration rates needs more explanation.
Fair attempt at conclusion.

Figure 4: Helen's completed infiltration experiment report.

Infiltration experiment   20th November

Aim:- to measure the infiltration rate of sand, soil and grass and test the hypothesis.

Hypothesis:- I think that sand will soak up water the fastest followed by soil then grass.

Method:- We carried out this experiment for homework, by getting either a tin can with both ends sawn off, or a length of plastic tubing. We were told to put our tube into the ground so only the top end is stick out of the ground.

Then we stuck a ruler in the tube and poured in some water, (I used 250 ml) and measure the length of time it takes the water to drop to a certain level, (I waited for it to drop 5cm). The time will differ with the different surfaces.

Figure 5: Samantha's completed infiltration experiment report.

Samantha's investigation compared with Helen's

It is useful to compare different students' performance on the same task. Figure 5 shows Samantha's second investigation in key stage 3, produced at the same time and with the same guidance as Helen's (Figure 4). Samantha's investigation shows glimpses of performance at the middle to top of the intermediate category on Figure 3: she has selected appropriate data presentation techniques for an awkward data set and she makes a good attempt to analyse the reasons for the variations in infiltration rates.

Helen's progress – year 9

During the course of the next year, Helen completed another three investigations and – at the end of the autumn term in year 9 – embarked upon her fifth with a greater degree of confidence and understanding of the enquiry process. She had been studying natural hazards and was given a student's study guide (Figure 6) and a guidance sheet on how to ask – and respond to – geographical questions (Figure 7). A criterion-referenced marking sheet for this investigation is shown in Figure 8. Note that because it is designed to assess a higher level investigation, with a wider range of possible outcomes, this marking sheet was much more

Student's study guide

This study guide explains how to go about completing your investigation. You should choose a case study from anywhere in the world to illustrate *one* of the following:

• earthquake; • volcanic eruption; • river flood.

The stages you should go through in your investigation are listed below:

1. write down the questions you want to answer, ready for your teacher's approval;

2. gather the evidence you need to answer your questions; write down where you intend to look, ready for your teacher's approval (see suggestions below); this stage may be completed in groups if you wish, but the next two stages must be individual work;

3 present and analyse your evidence, then evaluate your evidence and draw conclusions, do this by writing a report (no more than 500 words) with good use of graphs, maps and diagrams as appropriate; use as much IT as you wish and can obtain access to (word processing is greatly preferred for your text);

Suggestions for sources of evidence (see 2. above):

• conversations with family/friends/neighbours (particularly if you choose local floods);

• photographs from family/friends/neighbours (particularly if you choose flooding);

• school colour slides and filmstrips;

• textbooks in school library;

• local newspaper libraries (for floods, e.g. Jan/Feb 1990 or Dec 1994/Jan 1995);

• flood level markers on buildings and riversides;

• water companies (Welsh Water/Severn Trent);

• National Rivers Authorities;

• Local Authorities Emergency Planning Officer (South Herefordshire District/HWCC);

• CD-ROM *Times/Guardian* newspapers in supported self-study room;

• school videos;

• Encyclopaedias in school library or at home;

• Tony Crisp – *Rivers*;

• Tony Crisp – *Earthquakes and Volcanoes*;

• *GeoActive* case studies;

• *Wideworld* magazine articles;

• wall displays in geography classroom (access can be arranged out of lesson time).

Figure 6: Student's study guide for an investigation into a natural hazard and how people respond to it.

Asking geographical questions

You will be used to teachers asking you to answer *their* questions, but in geography you will be expected to learn how to ask *your own* geographical questions. These questions will be an important part of your pupil investigations. The guidelines below are designed to help you, so you should stick them securely into your exercise book. Show them to other people if you get stuck and a teacher is not around to help you.

Nearly all geographical questions will include at least one of the following key words:
what? where? how? who? why?

Geographers ask questions about almost anything – as you will find out! Some common things include:
patterns processes problems change appearance differences similarities interactions connections structure

Geographical questions are best kept short. If there are many things you wish to ask, you should ask several short questions rather than one big complicated one.

Here are some good examples of geographical questions:

• *What patterns* do river channels make (looked at from above)?
• *How* do rivers *wear away* the land?
• *Where* are there examples of rivers *wearing* away the land?
• *Who* might *be affected* by rivers *wearing away* the land?
• *What* can people do to *manage* rivers?

How to write a question-based investigation
Your approach will have to be different from the other type of investigation which is based on practical data collection to test an hypothesis. It is vital to start with a good set of questions (see above).

• You should gather all the evidence you think is relevant to your questions; make sure you include information about real places and cases, relevant graphs, maps, diagrams, tables, photographs, etc. It is much better – and cheaper and quicker – to make notes on those things which are relevant, rather than copying or printing large blocks of someone else's words (many of which will not be relevant to your question).
• Write down your first question, leave a line and write your answer in your own words. Develop your answer thoroughly* and organise it into separate sections if there are several points or strands to the answer. Make sure to support your answer with information about real places and cases and relevant graphs, maps, diagrams, tables, photographs, etc., on which you comment in your text.
• Repeat this procedure for each question in turn; there is no need to write an 'evaluation' section.
• Now critically read your own work, paying close attention to spelling, punctuation and grammar – make corrections as you go. This last stage can bring an enormous improvement to the quality of your investigation.

Note: * A thorough answer is one which directly addresses all aspects of the question and is supported with evidence from real places and cases. If you do not understand how to be thorough, ask your teacher to give you some examples.

Figure 7: Information on asking questions and writing a question-based investigation.

comprehensive than those used previously. Helen planned her investigation into landslides (Figure 9) and carried it out. Her work is shown in Figure 10, together with her teacher's comments. This time, Helen's teacher decided that her performance fits into the lower end of the 'advanced' category. In terms of 'places' she analyses the human and physical causes and effects of two major historical landslides (Aberfan and Vainont), and conveys a strong sense of place in her description of a recent landslide event which she has experienced.

The nature of her investigation means that the assessment criteria for 'patterns and processes' are not particularly appropriate, but she makes some important comments about environmental management ('environmental relationships and issues') in relation to Aberfan and her two local examples. In 'geographical enquiry and skills', Helen performs well: she manages to come up with her own questions with little guidance from her teacher; she selects from both primary and secondary data, and the use of 'before and after' photographs is a

Theme	Foundation (Levels 1-3)	Intermediate (Levels 4-6)	Advanced (Levels 7-Exceptional performance)
Places	Identifies and begins to offer observations about simple features of hazards in specific places; makes simple comparisons between features of hazard in different places.	Becoming aware of how physical and human processes interact in the hazard study area and that people have different views about this interaction (e.g. issues around Aberfan spoil heaps).	Appreciating how change in physical and/or human processes may be reflected in the changing character of places and how different viewpoints may influence decisions (e.g. issues around Aberfan spoil heaps).
Patterns and processes	Makes simple observations about patterns of chosen hazard and the processes which create it.	Identifies and describes patterns of chosen hazard and explains the process which create it and the effects it has on people and places.	Understanding how and why change may have impacts on people and places.
Environmental relationships and issues	Expressing mainly personal and subjective views about the chosen physical hazard; identifying and describing easily recognisable examples of the interactions between people and the environment and of attempts to manage these (e.g. urbanisation – flood control schemes).	Appreciating and finding evidence in a more objective way for the different views and opinions held by others, and recognising these as processes of change (e.g. Coal Board v. Aberfan families). Describing and offering explanations for different examples of environmental change with varied management responses (e.g. urbanization – flooding – flood control schemes).	Understanding the significance of different viewpoints in influencing environmental policy and decisions (e.g. Coal Board v. Aberfan families). Explaining the origins and character of complex issues and evaluating the impact of management strategies.
Geographical enquiry skills	Drawing on limited experiences and resources to answer simple geographical questions using basic vocabulary. Using simple techniques and undertaking straightforward tasks demonstrated by the teacher.	Drawing on their own experience to identify geographical questions, following a structured sequence of investigation and presenting a consistent geographical argument. Becoming aware of and selecting from a range of appropriate techniques, and demonstrating competence in using a wide range of geographical skills and vocabulary.	Demonstrating independence in posing appropriate questions, planning investigations and providing articulate and substantiated arguments. Demonstrating confidence in selecting skills and strategies appropriate to the task, and applying them effectively.

Figure 8: Physical hazard investigation assessment grid based on exemplification of standards. Source: SCAA, 1996.

good illustration of her selection of strategies appropriate to the task.

Possible developments

Other assessments, for example short tests or examinations, may be devised to allow students to show evidence of their attainment in the four aspects; these assessments will be kept in the portfolio.

The criterion-referenced marking sheets (Figures 3 and 8) are not readily comprehensible to students but it might be possible to develop a marking sheet which would be. The teacher might annotate or highlight this sheet and attach a copy to each student's work in order to help the student understand the assessment process, and what she or he needs to do in order to progress. An experimental sheet of this nature – for the natural hazards investigation – is included here (Figure 11).

THE JOHN KYRLE HIGH SCHOOL GEOGRAPHY DEPARTMENT

Pupil's investigation planning sheet

Pupil's name: Helen Chamberlain   Landslides

Write down your questions or hypotheses:

What causes landslides?
Where have they happened?   use case-studies + local maps
How do they effect people?
How do they deal with them after they happen?   people
Why do landslides happen? x   Can people be
    same as 1   protected or landslides
                                     prevented
teacher approval (initials): NJM   date: 27-12-96

Write down how you intend to collect your evidence:

I will speak to parents and neighbours.
I will collect Newspaper evidence.
I will look in books.

What help do you need?:

Figure 9: Helen's completed investigation
planning sheet for 'Landslides'.

The QCA (1998) discussion paper *Geographical
Enquiry at Key Stages 1-3* contains other models of
assessment, for example, the planning framework
for a year 9 coursework task (Figure 12).

A workable process

The examples here illustrate the assessment of
individual student investigations. They are given in
order to exemplify the *assessment process* rather than
standards of achievement. Moreover, we should not
be directed into considering too closely the levels
assigned to the students' work in this chapter, or
notions of national standards. These will take some
years for classroom teachers to determine. What is
important is that this chapter presents a move
towards a workable key stage 3 assessment process
which enables us to:

- understand what we are assessing,
  and why;
- plan appropriate assessment opportunities;
- justify the assessment decisions we
  are making;
- engage in formative assessment
  with students;
- monitor students' progress;
- empower students by teaching them the
  transferable skill of enquiry.

(1)

Natural Hazards
          Landslides

Questions – What causes landslides?
    Where have they happened?
    How do they effect people?
    How do people deal with one af
    they occurs?

Aim – The aim of this investigation is to answ
these questions including case studies and
evidence collected from books and friend
and family.

Evidence – Landslides are caused by a
number of different things, some are natura
and some are man-inflicted.
Some of these things are:-

① A very hot summer which causes
    cracks in a slope, then the heavy ra
    in autumn and other storms and
    there is a build up of pressure in
    the crack and it pushes the soil
    forwards.

② The cutting down of trees affects the
    amount of water hitting the groun
    Once most of the water would hav
    stopped at the leaves but when
    they are cut down the water satur
    the ground and it slips.

Figure 10: Helen's 'Landslides' report. This was illustrated with cop
photographs, but these are omitted here.

(3)

The landslide that occured at Bracken Bank
could have been hazardous.
It was caused by the ground cracking and
then the water making pressure in the
cracks, so the soil fell.
    It happened in Feb 1990 and the soil etc.
slid straight into the back of the house.
Luckily no-one was hurt but while everything
was being rebuilt the whole family had
to move somewhere else.

(4)

Roughly 4000 tons of soil was removed
after the bank fell.
The owners had metal (girders) put   girders
vertically against the bank then they
dropped railway sleepers behind the (girders)
to try to stop it falling again.
But Unfortunatly the pressure was too
great and the weight of it all bent over the
girders and a smaller landslide occured.
This time they built a retaining wall
and this was successful.

③ The removal of vegetation which was holding the soil in place, when it is taken away the soil moves.

what sort of 'debris'?

④ If debris is put on a slope and the ground can't cope with the weight it might slip.

⑤ A small earthquake or a series of small earthquakes may cause a landslide.

These things may not necessarily cause a landslide every time they happen.

→ S. Wales

Some places that landslides have occured are Aberfan, Bracken Bank-Coppett Hill, Main Road on Coppett Hill next to Charlton and and a side of the Vaiont Resevoir (Italy?)

Yorkshire

Aberfan was described as one of the biggest psychological disasters since the war.
It happened at 9.30am on the 21st October 1966
7 slag heaps were built on top of a stream, it rained for 4 days and all the *extra* water loosened the tip of one of them and it fell.
The school and nearby dwellings were engulfed by thousands of tonnes of waste shale.

---

(2) Everyone pitched in to help dig out the 130 people entombed. All the emergency services were there and also the Red Cross etc. The bodies of children and adults were crushed beyond recognition, it was well into the second week when the police knew the final death total.
It was 144, 116 children and 28 adults.

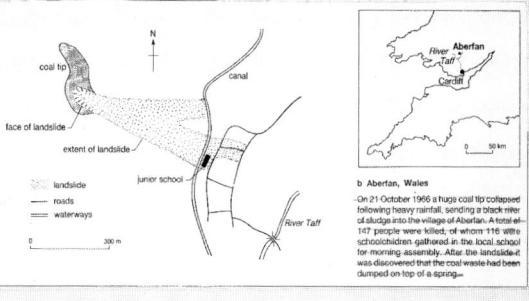

b Aberfan, Wales
On 21 October 1966 a huge coal tip collapsed following heavy rainfall, sending a black river of sludge into the village of Aberfan. A total of 147 people were killed, of whom 116 were schoolchildren gathered in the local school for morning assembly. After the landslide it was discovered that the coal waste had been dumped on top of a spring.

There was a tribunal that lasted 6 months, the blame was finally fixed on the national coal board for building *tips* on the stream and for not doing proper maintenance on them.
The 6 other slag heaps were removed with the £150,000 donated by people.

(which caused some resentment!)

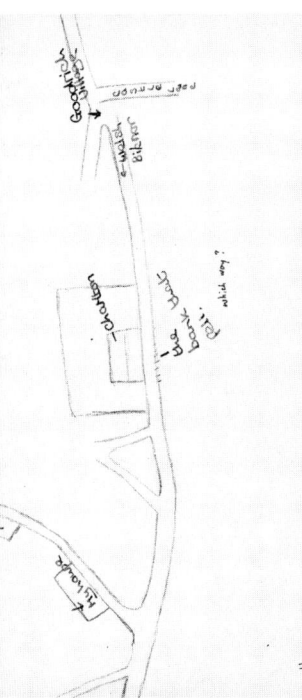

The landslide on the main road of Coppett Hill next to the house Charlton could have been disastrous aswell, but luckily no-one was hurt.
~~In 1992 at Christmas time the side of the road fell away and pieces of rubble appeared in our field by the road~~
It was caused by the pressure of water in a crack that had opened up during the summer.
There were drains going to the outside of the bank that might have prevented the landslide (because the water would have just flowed away down the bank) if the council had cleaned them out.
The council then left it a year before doing anything serious about it.
They drove interlocking metal piles into the ground to hold everything back.

The last landslide that I am about to report on was massive and it had disastrous effects.
It happened on the 9th October 1963.
2 months of heavy rain and many small earthquakes *were* the causes of the steep southern side of the Vaiont Resevoir in Italy falling.
240,000,000 cubic metres of earth, rocks etc fell into the Resevoir in less than 30 secs. This created huge waves, they topped the dam by 100 metres and crashed down in the valleys below.
Over 2,600 people were killed.

7
8
9

---

(6) **Conclusions** - Some landslides are harmless but others can be really dangerous, it's really just luck sometime whether anybody gets hurt or not.
Some landslides could be prevented if people would to the maintenance jobs they are paid to do.
~~Landslides~~ aren't necessarily 'natural hazards'.
ie. some are caused by peoples activities.

A good investigation which is very much your own work. It hangs together very well and covers a wide range of points about landslides. Well done.

7/6   ✓MERITS✓

Good use of case studies (including local/personal)
Good comment on management
Uses own questions
Appropriate data presentation choices
Note detailed comment on improving your written communication of ideas.

written

Theme	Foundation (Levels 1-3)	Intermediate (Levels 4-6)	Advanced (Levels 7- Exceptional performance)
Places	Refers to specific places.	Refers to a range of named, located specific places.	Consistently exemplifies points with reference to a wide range of named located specific places.
Patterns and processes	Simply describes effect(s) of hazard upon people's lives.	Describes and explains features and hazard in terms of processes operating.	Draws together relationships across several scales.
Environmental relationships and issues	Expressing mainly personal and subjective views about the chosen physical hazard; identifying and describing easily recognisable examples of the interactions between people and the environment and of attempts to manage these (e.g. urbanisation – flood control schemes).	Appreciating and finding evidence in a more objective way for the different views and opinions held by others, and recognising these as processes of change (e.g. Coal Board v. Aberfan families). Describing and offering explanations for different examples of environmental change with varied management responses (e.g. urbanization – flooding – flood control schemes).	Understanding the significance of different viewpoints in influencing environmental policy and decisions (e.g Coal Board v. Aberfan families). Explaining the origins and character of complex issues and evaluating the impact of management strategies.
Enquiry skills			
Questions	Uses teacher's questions	Comes up with own questions	Original and imaginative questions
Evidence	Uses small range of sources selected by teacher	Uses a range of sources taken from those held in school	Wide range of sources of evidence used from inside and outside the school
Guidance	Follows teacher's instructions step-by-step	Follows general structure for enquiry	Comes up with original topic and/or structure with little or no teacher guidance
Data presentation	Presents data as directed by teacher	Chooses range of appropriate presentation techniques	Produces a wide range of data presentation techniques (e.g. text, photos, maps, tables)
Written communication	Simple language/brief/many SPG errors	Wider vocabulary including some geographical terms/more thorough development of ideas/occasional SPG errors	Advanced written communication skills with wide vocabulary, including geographical terms/complex analysis/rare SPG errors

Figure 11: Mark sheet for year 9 students' investigations into a chosen natural hazard.

Medium-term assessment: Professional development activities

1. Review your medium-term (unit) plans for key stage 3 or key stage 4; identify a key

assessment opportunity within each one. Review the assessment opportunities across the key stage as a whole:

• How far do these assessment opportunities promote attainment by

Year 9 Unit 3 'The changing industrial scene': South Wales

Coursework task: South Wales: the place to be!

Task

Produce a leaflet/poster which sells South Wales as a place to locate a modern hi-tech factory for a company from the Far East which wants to build a factory in Europe, e.g. Lucky Gold Star, a South Korean company, wanting to build a multi-million pound factory at Newport.

Some example selling points for South Wales could be:

• New factory sites next to M4 motorway, easy access to Midlands via M5, and to Europe.

• Two hours from Heathrow airport via M4.

• Sites available with services/facilities.

• Skilled, flexible workforce.

• Good quality of life – near countryside, e.g. Brecon Beacons.

• The role of the WDA attracting business to South Wales.

Level 3	**Level 5**	**Level 7**
Description	**Explanation**	**Rationalisation**
A Level 3 answer would be largely descriptive and not develop/explain the value of each selling point/reason for choosing Newport.	A Level 5 response would mention links between economic and social factors. It would discuss the role of the WDA in attracting industry to South Wales – for example, help in planning and the inducements offered. A Level 5 answer would show 'plausible conclusions and present findings both graphically and in writing'.	A Level 7 answer would give consideration to several selling points including social, economic and maybe even cultural factors (hospitable people). The role of the WDA would be discussed, including its value as a whole to South Wales. A Level 7 answer would show that students are 'beginning to reach substantiated conclusions'.

Figure 12: The planning framework for a coursework assessment task.
Note: This task is based on a real example; the decision was made in 1996. Source: QCA, 1998.

involving a wide range of students, for example, through a variety of assessment strategies?
• How far do they provide access to all aspects of attainment?
• How far do they ensure progression, e.g. in enquiry?

2. Discuss how you can use these key assessment opportunities to provide feedback to students on their strengths and areas for improvement:
• How will you use these to set targets with students and monitor their progress and success?

3. How will the assessment opportunities and feedback inform, and help you amend, your plans:
• For the following work?
• For the same unit next year?

4. Using the QCA units as a model, discuss your expectations for key aspects of attainment, studying one of your own geography topics or units. Start with what you expect the majority of students to attain, then modify these to produce expectations for students attaining more, and less, than the majority.

Photo: Roger Carter.

Chapter 6

Long-term, summative assessment and evaluation: portfolios

- **How can portfolios of students' work support assessment in geography?**

The main issues explored within this chapter are that:

- **while there is no obligation on schools or departments to collect students' work into portfolios, they are useful for a number of reasons;**
- **the role of portfolio can be developed in different ways, but school or departmental portfolios are especially useful for monitoring progression in achievement and 'standards';**
- **at key stage 3, portfolios are a priority in supporting the process of reporting a level in year 9.**

Evidence in geography

An important purpose of recording is to collect evidence of students' experiences and achievements in geography, in order to: track progress and set targets for improvement, demonstrate attainment during the key stage (for example when reporting annually to parents), and support end-of-key stage judgements. The range of evidence available in geography is considerable (Figure 1), and it is good practice to plan for as much variety as possible, to help students to demonstrate positive achievement. *Exemplifications of Standards* (SCAA, 1996a) provides useful support for this process.

Geography portfolios

A portfolio is a collection of student's work and other material which exemplifies standards of work in a school or department. At key stage 3, it is the basis on which level judgements are made in geography within a school.

There is no statutory requirement for schools to produce portfolios of any kind. However, many schools choose to do so because they consider portfolio development to be good practice. Some people may use the term 'record of learning outcomes' (ROLO) instead of 'portfolio'. This chapter illustrates how the role of the portfolio has developed among teachers, before demonstrating how it is being used in one geography department.

Retainable evidence

1. Direct evidence (responses to enquiry questions, in writing or other geographical ways):

- a range of writing for different purposes: story, letter, extended writing, notes, drafts, display, newspaper article, story board, ICT;
- a range of visual materials: maps, photographs, pictures, diagrams, graphs, sketches, models, video, ICT;
- data response items;
- responses by individuals, pairs, groups.

2. Indirect evidence

- student review sheet demonstrating geographical achievement;
- teacher observations/notes, e.g. fieldwork tasks.

Ephemeral evidence

- Oral, for example, presentation as a result of individual or group work.
- Role play in decision-making exercises, e.g. related to a controversial issue.

Figure 1: Types of evidence in geography. Adapted from: GAIN (no date).

Types of portfolio

Several different types of portfolio are currently being developed in schools.

Whole school/departmental/key stage portfolios are intended to provide a focus for promoting consistent judgements about levels of achievement and exemplifying a school's standards. They can help provide feedback for curriculum evaluation and review.

Individual student portfolios are likely to contain a small sample of evidence to underpin, exemplify and provide confidence in more summative records. As such they may provide a focus for discussion, e.g. with parents and students (see below), and support the reporting process.

Class portfolios can help accountability by demonstrating that the planned curriculum has indeed been taught. They can also serve as a focus for curriculum evaluation and review.

School or departmental portfolios

'A school portfolio contains pieces of work and teachers' observations that have been assessed and agreed by the teachers in the school. It is helpful to include samples that exemplify attainment at each level including borderlines between level ... most schools already have samples that have been assessed collectively at agreement trials or staff meetings and these can form the basis of a portfolio. Once school portfolios are established, it is important to review them regularly' (Dearing, 1995, pp. 105-6).

School or departmental portfolios are collections of work exemplifying standards and attainment in relation to the key stage programme of study. They have a range of audiences, which include:

- **student: feedback and feedforward**
- **parents**
- **colleagues**
- **new teachers**
- **new school**
- **senior management**
- **college, further education institution, etc.**
- **advisers/inspectors**

Portfolios also have a range of purposes, for example, they can:

- **serve as a reference point for all teachers in promoting and supporting consistent judgements both during a key stage and at the end of a key stage;**
- **be used as a focus for moderation between schools;**
- **support new colleagues in informing their understanding and judgements;**

- **remove the pressure on individual teachers to build up their own collection of work to support their judgements;**
- **demonstrate to others (e.g. parents, other teachers, students, governors, Ofsted) the agreed standards of work within the school;**
- **exemplify progression and support evaluation and review of the school's geography curriculum;**
- **include work from a small number of 'case study' students, showing a range of work and attainment, for example, Levels 3, 5 and 7.**

A portfolio can include either one student's work at a range of levels, to exemplify how 'best fit' judgements are reached, or collections of work from different students which, taken together, help teachers understand achievement in a particular aspect of the programme of study. The materials can include:

Name:	Date:
Topic/unit	POS/objectives

Context: (description of learning activity, degree of support)

Who chose this piece of work?

What features of attainment does this work show? Why has it been selected?

What (if anything) does this work fail to demonstrate?

Next steps

Figure 2: Sample commentary sheet.

- students' written work, artefacts, photographs, audio or video tapes;
- at key stage 3, students' responses to SCAA/ACAC task materials;
- students' self-assessment records or logs, validated by the teacher;
- extracts from teacher records, markbooks or notes of ephemeral, practical, visual or other evidence.

To be most useful, materials in portfolios need a commentary sheet from the class teacher to establish the context of the work and the nature of the attainment (Figure 2). Commentaries might include:

- explanations of a context or focus for samples of work;
- annotation to indicate agreed features of performance in pieces of work;
- a summary showing how the work fulfils expectations;
- a brief explanation of why judgements were made and how the materials support them.

Experience with school/departmental portfolios suggests it is better to provide a small number of case study students and a more detailed commentary, rather than many students in less depth. Adequate staff development time needs to be allocated for the agreement discussions; do not rush the process or set unrealistic targets. Portfolios can be compiled over time and reviewed or supplemented annually.

The development of a departmental portfolio for key stage 3 is necessary for three reasons:

- The requirement to report a level at the end of year 9 means that all teachers in a department need to focus to reach a common understanding of the level descriptions, and to agree common judgements in relation to them.

- It is clear that the level descriptions can only be applied to the body of work produced by a student over several years. The summative nature of the level descriptions is made clear by the frequent use of the phrase 'range of' within them. Year 9 teachers, who are responsible for determining and reporting the student's level, should have access to a selection of 'benchmark' judgements, agreed with all members of the department, to help make level judgements about all students in their year 9 groups.

- Student achievement in the enquiry process is a major component of the level descriptions (and a focus of Ofsted inspections). Individual student investigations (enquiries) throughout key stage 3 can be planned and carried out, then the students' work and the teacher commentaries annotated and placed in the portfolio. At the end of key stage 3, the student's teacher reviews the whole portfolio and assigns a level on a 'best-fit' basis using the level descriptions.

SCAA and ACAC's exemplification materials, produced to support the process of making judgements at the end of key stage 3 (SCAA, 1996; ACAC, 1996), show what a departmental portfolio might contain and how it could be organised, as well as indicating national expectations about levels. QCA's discussion paper on geographical enquiry also gives useful examples of portfolio material (QCA, 1998).

Departmental portfolios have a key role in establishing level descriptions for geography, reaching common agreement across the department and applying these judgements meaningfully to individual students' attainments. Where possible, portfolios can also provide a useful focus for discussion of standards among schools, for example in consortia groups or across local education authorities.

Individual or class portfolios

These portfolios usually contain a small sample of students' work to support the class teacher's judgements about student progress. For example, teachers might keep one piece of work from each student for each geography topic or unit, involving a whole-year group activity which has been identified as providing good evidence of students' attainment. This would be a manageable, useful and systematic way of recording and monitoring attainment and progress for the following reasons:

- **a focus on common assessment activities enables comparison across teaching groups (and, potentially, from year to year), aiding monitoring and evaluation;**
- **these portfolios fit in with ideas about records of achievement and could include an element of student self-assessment;**
- **individual portfolios can provide useful information for reporting to parents or the following teacher;**
- **a small sample from each year's portfolio could be retained to feed into the key stage (school or department) portfolio. Collecting work from three students at the top, middle and bottom of the ability range gives useful evidence for curriculum monitoring and evaluation.**

Constructing individual student portfolios can become an unwieldy and time-consuming process. However, developing portfolios in this way can engage students in the assessment process in a meaningful way and contribute to the development of a 'truly formative assessment regime' (Lambert, 1997).

Portfolios – decisions to be made

Staff involvement
Who will lead/co-ordinate the work?
Who will be involved in the development of the portfolio?
How will the department ensure that the portfolio represents the agreed interpretations of teachers in the school?

Coverage
What range of levels will be included?
Which year group(s) will be represented?

Timescale for development and review
What is the timescale for development?
When will the review begin?
What forms will it take and who will do it?

Range and type of material
What kind of materials will be included:
• samples from a range of students' work?
• sample sets of work by individual students?
• SCAA/ACAC exemplification materials, or optional test and task material?

Type and extent of commentary
How much, and what kind of commentary or annotation is needed? For example, will it provide a context for the work, a brief explanation of why a judgement was made?

Case study: John Kyrle High School

This section illustrates the individual portfolio work of the Geography Department at the John Kyrle High School.

What types of work go into the individual student portfolio?

Students build up their portfolios on their individual investigation work. They carry out ten investigations across key stage 3. Each investigation is an integral part of the course and comes in the form of homework at the end of a unit of study. Students produce their investigations on separate sheets of A4 paper. Each student is given:

- a general guide to undertaking and presenting an investigation (see Chapter 5, Figures 2 and 7);
- a study guide specific to the investigation in question (see Chapter 5, Figure 6);
- an investigation planning sheet (see Chapter 5, Figure 9).

This method of work has exposed the need to keep adapting the approach. The initial selection of investigations may have left some areas of the level descriptions relatively 'bare', so the next step will be to compare the content of the level descriptions with the assessment opportunities presented by the investigations. A key point is ensuring that the investigations in year 9 are more demanding than those in year 7; a student's progress in investigative work is a formative process. Students' performance in other forms of key assessment (e.g. annual examinations) is retained in their portfolios. The portfolio might also include teachers' notes and observations of learning, and records of ephemeral activities, e.g. photographs from fieldwork.

How are the investigations marked and annotated?

The most important part of the marking process is the comment on how the student should aim to improve. This underlines the formative nature of assessment using portfolios. Teachers extend the formative element by asking each student to complete a self-evaluation sheet (Figure 3). Students like to have a mark at the end of their work, so at present teachers write a comment and/or attach a mark sheet to the work (see Chapter 5, Figure 11), with an indication of the level achieved. (The students understand that one piece of work is insufficient to determine a definitive level.) This marking system is another point for discussion and adaptation because of the difficulty of applying summative level descriptions to individual pieces of work. It is important that marks (levels) for individual pieces of work are recorded against a class list in the teacher's mark book (in case of loss or damage to work in the portfolio).

The year 9 teacher has the task of making 'the big decision' on a student's level at the end of key stage 3 and it will be the year 9 work which provides the main basis for this decision. The function of the earlier work is to provide the breadth necessary to meet the level descriptions and also to build up the student's skills, knowledge and understanding. The student's achievement in terms of breadth, describing, explaining, recognising, and enquiry are all considered on a 'best-fit' basis against the level descriptions. Work outside the portfolio is also taken into consideration, such as a student's oral responses.

Where are the portfolios kept?

In each geography classroom there is a bank of lockers for each class to store their portfolios. Another method (in an average-size school) would be to use a filing cabinet, in which one drawer holds one year group's portfolios, divided into teaching groups. Every time a piece of work is marked and returned, the student files it in her or his portfolio – a cardboard A4 pocket folder – and reviews previous work and self-evaluations.

Student's Name: _____ Date: _____

Investigation title: _____

_____

Did you understand what you had to do? _____

_____

What did you find difficult? _____

_____

_____

What did you enjoy? _____

_____

_____

Do you understand the teacher's comments and/or mark? _____

_____

What do you have to do, to make progress in the future? _____

_____

Figure 3: The student's geography self-evaluation sheet.
(The John Kyrle High School).

What is the students' response to working in this way?

Students like the idea that the portfolio is theirs and that it is a growing record
of their achievement. They also like working on separate sheets of paper rather
than in the usual exercise books, and many of them make good use of word-
processing and desktop publishing. They enjoy producing something which they
own and value. Each student will take away the portfolio at the end of key stage
3. A student may remove individual marked pieces of work to show at home, on
the understanding that loss of the work will deplete the portfolio.

What about other student work?

The department's units of study cover the whole programme of study through the classwork and homework which continues throughout the three years and is written in the students' exercise books. Each student is responsible for the exercise book, which is available for reference during investigations and for revision before annual school examinations.

Photo: Margaret Roberts.

What about the departmental portfolio?

In the summer, after departmental moderation of key stage 3 levels, portfolios which indicate achievement at each level are selected. These are copied and retained as a single departmental portfolio for future reference. The department's portfolio is being updated as the years pass and the levels become more clearly established. This clarification of levels involves local and national consultation over published results.

Are there additional advantages?

- One great advantage of the student portfolio is that it can be forwarded to a new school if a student moves home, providing the new teacher with a valuable indication of the standard of the student's work. The same is true if a student moves between teaching groups during the school year.

- The individual portfolio approach also covers much of the ground which preoccupies Ofsted inspectors, for example, assessment policy, enquiry-based learning, formative assessment and student involvement in the assessment process.

- The portfolios are readily available for occasions when students or parents need to be consulted about progress.

- The investigative process is at the heart of the coursework component of GCSE and A-level examinations. Teachers are hopeful that students' success with key stage 3 investigations will lead to success in their external examinations, and encourage them to carry on studying geography.

- Other departments in the school have shown an interest in the geography department's methods of assessment.

- Portfolios can support new colleagues in informing their understanding and judgements.

- The skills of investigation, report writing and presentation of work in a portfolio are sought by employers.

Professional development activities

1. Collect pieces of current or past work from a few individual students which you think exemplify two different levels within the key stage. Check these against the appropriate level (or grade) descriptions. Discussion: How useful were the pieces of work?

2.a. Audit your key stage 3 schemes of work to identify a range of key assessment opportunities which together:

   • cover the range of knowledge, understanding and skills referred to in the level descriptions

   • provide access to the various key elements.

b. Come to an agreement about the types of work you wish to target to build up your portfolio.

3.a. Audit the results of your moderated end of key stage 3 level judgements against the four aspects of attainment in geography. What does this tell you about departmental strengths and weaknesses in teaching the programmes of study?

b. Now translate the weaknesses into key curriculum targets, e.g. understanding of places, and identify the relevant medium-term (unit) plans where you need to take action.

Photo: Sally and Richard Greenhill.

Chapter 7

Long-term, summative assessment and evaluation: departmental examinations and target setting

- **What are the key points to remember when devising internal examinations?**
- **How can good practice in assessment contribute to the process of target setting?**

The main issues explored within this chapter are that:

- departmental examinations can make an important contribution to an assessment policy, but to make these a positive experience for students takes thought and skill;
- examiners' reports and end of key stage 3 moderation can provide valuable information to help target getting;
- a good system of assessment is an essential basis for meaningful target setting.

Setting internal examinations

Most schools have an examination week each year. Not all subjects have timed, written papers but geography usually does. Even when teachers have enough evidence from the course to set targets and report to parents, the examination may be retained to give the subject status. However, a badly set examination lowers the status of geography in the eyes of the students. Few teachers have had any training in setting internal examinations and their experience of examinations set by 'professionals' may be limited to GCSE and A-level papers. Are these appropriate templates for lower school examinations?

Can a common paper extend the more able students and be accessible to the less able?

At 16, students will face not a common examination paper but Higher Tier, Foundation Tier or Certificate of Achievement. Likewise, in key stage 3 the style of questions and the language used should match ability. The less able students need more structure and do not cope well with choice. A shorter examination, matching concentration span, should be considered. A good examination is a positive experience, allowing the students to exhibit how much they know, understand and can do. A common examination can leave the brightest frustrated at the lack of opportunity to develop their ideas, while the weakest go away with reinforced feelings of failure. Questions with very high or very low facilities (degree of difficulty) do not make any worthwhile contribution to the measurement of a student's ability.

What format should the examination paper take?

A question and answer booklet can be easy to mark. It also guides students so that they do not miss questions out and indicates the length of response required. However, non-consumable question papers and lined paper are not only cheaper, they also allow more able students to extend their answers.

A teacher's handwriting can be a hurdle to some students. Type the examination paper, and space out the questions. No matter how simple the tasks, densely packed pages are more difficult to read and will put students off. Lay it out attractively to encourage attractive answers.

Why bother with a mark scheme?

Putting the mark scheme together checks the viability of the questions – ambiguities are identified and mark allocation verified. (There is no point in allocating four marks for a question which asks for reasons, at one mark each, if you can only think of three reasons.) Mark schemes must be flexible, allowing for the unexpected. Lower school geography is often added to the timetable of non-specialist staff, who greatly appreciate a mark scheme. A scheme's main advantage, though, is its value in achieving consistency of marking, enabling comparability between students. Feedback to students using the mark scheme can be very productive too. Try devising the mark scheme first, then setting the questions to match it!

What makes a good set of questions?

Students should feel that the questions actually link to the work done. They may not know the answers, but they know that each question is answerable! The examination should have a good mix of knowledge, understanding and skills tasks. It is worth allocating questions or marks to these three types of task when setting the paper.

Vary the structure for different abilities. Whatever the range of ability being tested, the first part may be short and relatively easy as a 'warm up' and confidence

booster for students. There may then be a sorting of questions to produce an incline of difficulty, with the most demanding last.

If students are to gain credit for producing examples in an answer, don't rely on telepathy – ask for them! Avoid questions with long preambles, they can distract from the real requirement. For example, if there is too much introductory information about a central business district in a question about the height of buildings, some students will simply describe the CBD. Students can also be hindered by complex wording. It is often better to break a question up into a statement followed by 'Why is this?'. If a question changes context part way through, it is better to make the second half a separate question. For example, if a question about industry in an MEDC ends by asking students to choose, describe and explain an LEDC industry, it will produce an MEDC example from some students.

Giving a choice of questions to middle and low ability students is hard to justify. Apart from the difficulties of making the questions of comparable difficulty, the first is likely to be the most popular, the last the least popular. Use command words that students will understand. 'Discuss' to many lower school students, means 'find somebody to talk to', probably not what you want during the exam! Some of these issues are summarised in Figure 1.

Does it have to be a written examination?

Students who may be impressive orally do not necessarily find it easy to express what they know and understand on paper. In reports to parents many teachers do acknowledge the oral contributions the students make, but this is often not formally assessed. Practical limitations mean that individual oral examinations are not usually feasible, although students could be assessed on their contributions to a whole-class discussion or role-play exercise. Oral assessment could be used selectively (such as with lower ability groups only) and may benefit from having a mark scheme.

Command word does not require the identification of the reasons, but strictly needs the pupil to show why the reasons are valid.

No indication of how many.

Option within the question.

Difficult word.

The first draft

3. Explain the reasons why <u>it was thought a good idea to designate</u> this area, or a similar area of your choice as land for either residential or industrial development and why some people, especially those living in the area <u>might have been less happy</u> about it.   [6]

46 word sentence!

Underlined sections particularly wordy.

A second option within the question.

More than one instruction within the question.

Reading age: Flesch – Kincard Grade level – 21.6
(Standard readability 7.0 – 8.0)

The amended question

Structured to take the pupil through in stages

3 a) Choose an area where **residential** or **industrial** development is planned. It could be the area on the map above.

Choices in print.

Part a) needed to show the context for b) and c).

i) Identify the area.

Clearer Command Words

ii) State the type of development.   [0]

b) Describe **two features** which make this a good location for the development.   [4]

Specifies how many.

Number in bold print.

c) Some people, especially local people, may not be happy about the development. Why is this?   [2]

Preamble and task separate.

A more student friendly font than the first draft.

Mark allocation could be shown as [6], allowing flexibility to reward development of answers.

Reading age: Flesch – Kincard Grade level – 7.2

Figure 1: How a question was improved.

Student self-assessment is growing in popularity and frequency of use. It can provide a valuable opportunity for students to assess their academic achievement, effort, strengths and weaknesses, and to set targets for improvement. In this way, self-assessment can aid the formative role of internal examinations.

Evaluation and review: using the Chief Examiner's report

Every year (more often for modular syllabuses) the Chief Examiner prepares a report on how candidates performed. A copy is sent to each school or college which entered candidates. Although it is written for teachers, it always contains information which will be helpful to future candidates. There is usually a general section which takes an overview and highlights common strengths and weaknesses, followed by separate commentaries on each question and on the coursework element. The final section may give statistical information about the marks needed and the proportion of candidates achieving each grade.

The general section often contains useful guidance which could apply to many subjects and syllabuses. It is worth looking at reports from other syllabuses and picking out points of generic wisdom, for example:

> 'There was an increase in the number of candidates who underlined what they considered to be the key words or phrases in the question. This helped them to focus on what the question wanted, although they still needed knowledge and understanding to guarantee quality of response. Many also adopted the good practice of pencilling in short plans in the margins for the longer answers, which helped them to compose more fluent responses with fuller coverage' (from A-level report).

The commentary on individual questions usually makes sense only if read alongside the question and is of most use just after the mock examinations. The positive identification of what made good answers is valuable, for example:

> 'In part (c), few made use of the photograph but most gained some credit for referring to access and room for expansion. The better candidates added cost of land, catchment area and competition to their analysis' (from GCSE report).

The statistical information can also be used after the mock examination to identify the grade which the candidate would have achieved on each paper. It is also possible to see how close the mark was to the threshold for the next grade up. Knowing which component of the assessment is weakest means that revision can be targeted.

Using case study examination answers

Figure 2 (pages 76-7), showing two GCSE candidates' scripts, can be used as a basis for classroom discussion and in a marking exercise. Students will understand what examiners are looking for and how a case study question is marked, and will see what happens if they do not answer the question.

Students could be asked:

- which candidate scored 9/9 and which scored 3/9?
- why did the examiner allocate marks like this?
- did both candidates understand the term landform?
- did both candidates focus clearly on trigger words, such as describe, management and good and bad effects?
- how many marks are/should be knocked off if candidates quote a river or dam (neither acceptable as a landform) rather than a river valley which is a landform?

Photo: Margaret Roberts.

Mark scheme for case study (section (d) of question C5)

d) Any natural landform permissible, e.g. river valley, flood plain, section of coast, estuary. Do not allow a river as opposed to river valley. Answers must discuss landforms, management and good/bad effects.

Annotate (d) for description and (e) for effects.
(i)   Description of how landform is being managed (maximum 5 for description)
(ii) Good/bad effects (maximum 4)

Not named or located – maximum 5.

Examiner's report

The candidate who chose the North Norfolk coast scored 9/9, while the candidate who chose to write about the Aswan Dam gained 3/9 marks.

North Norfolk cliffs

This candidate clearly understood what a landform is, and quoted an appropriate case study. The examiner used a tick with a 'd' to credit description marks, and a tick with an 'e' for any good or bad effects. In the first section 'd' marks were awarded for each strategy mentioned: 'man [sic] made protection strategies, gabion boxes, revetment, seawalls, redirect energy to the sea' Max 5 marks awarded to the candidate as there was evidence of expansion of points relating to how it was being managed. Award of 'e' marks was made with reference to prevention of slumping (good) in the first section; robbing another area of sand (bad), the cliffs are stabilised (good), bad effects on tourism and making beach look unattractive (bad). (Other good and bad effects were quoted but max marks had already been awarded.) This comment could be optional to share with students.

Aswan Dam

The candidate did not understand what a landform is. The Aswan Dam was quoted as the area but was also interpreted as the landform. A dam is neither a landform nor natural. As the candidate went on to mention the delta, and by implication refer to effects within the river valley (which is a landform), the max 3 marks for effects were allowed for reference to making more money from increased harvests (good), holding back silt which had allowed the delta to be eroded more (bad). No marks were allocated for describing the management of a landform as the candidate used an inappropriate choice here.

The examiner's report noted that the case study section of question C5 was answered very badly for three reasons:
1. *candidates do not appear to know what constitutes a natural landform;*
2. *candidates do not appear to bring good examples to the examination room. They appear unable to describe a landform and how it affects or is affected by people, as expected by the syllabus;*
3. *candidates' choice of case studies are particularly poor here.*
Source: Battersby et al., 1995.

(d) **Case Study**

For a named area describe how a natural landform (or landforms) is being managed by people. Describe the good and bad effects this management has had. Do not use examples from this question.

Name of the area   ~~Natu~~ Norfolk Coast — Cliffs

(i) Description of how the landform is being managed

The cliffs are very eroded and so man-made protection strategies are being used: ①GABION BOXES - to help support the cliffs and to try and prevent slumping. ②REVETMENTS, timber constructions at 45° angle on beach to absorb shock of waves, yet let water through ③SEA-WALL - to take force of wave power, and to also redirect the energy to the sea. ④adding boulders and sand to the beach ⑤GROYNES - timber 'walls' going out towards the sea to allow the beach to build up to protect beach against longshore drift. ⑥RESTRICTING ACCESS to people so they don't walk on cliffs.

(ii) Good and bad effects

⊕That area is kind of protected-but, ⊖for example with groynes that sand would go somewhere else + so is robbing another area; ⊕The cliffs are stabalised; ⊖Very expensive and often you need more than one type of protection. ⊖bad effect on tourism, as with many they make the beach unattractive + you can't see the water - as with revetments, having a knock on effect on tourist industry + it declines. ⊕Beach is built up by groynes, which may boost the tourist industry ⊖Major disadvantage is that other areas are robbed from protection that the eroded/LSD sand would have given them ⊖They (the protections) get worn away themselves + need other strategies to save them. [9]

END OF QUESTION C5   [Total 36 marks]

Figure 2: (a) candidate A's response.

(d)   Case Study

For a named area describe how a natural landform (or landforms) is being managed by people.   Describe the good and bad effects this management has had.   Do not use examples from this question.

Name of the area   Aswan Dam

(i)   Description of how the landform is being managed

A dam has been built to control the discharge of water and to make the flow consistent all year round. As the snow melted from the mountains the river would flood providing the Egyptian Fellah with a harvest. This was too unreliable as the water did not come in controlled amounts. Now the flow can be controlled to give harvests all year round

(ii)   Good and bad effects

The Fellah had a more successful business and could make more money from the harvests. It also held up a disease called BILHARZIA which comes in the water.

Unfortunately it held up the natural fertiliser — SILT. This meant the fellahs had to pay for fertiliser and also the Delta became eroded. The sardine fishermen suffered because it held up the nutrients which [9] the fish fed on and they died.   [Total 36 marks]

END OF QUESTION C5

Figure 2: (b) candidate B's response.

Target setting and target getting

Target setting

Target setting is now a national requirement for maintained schools. In secondary schools, the targets are currently related to improving GCSE grades at key stage 4. Some local education authorities and schools have chosen to set additional optional targets, for example, raising the percentage of students achieving Level 6 and above at key stage 3. Whatever they are, geography departments will need to contribute to setting the targets, and getting the targets. Central to this is the teachers' professional judgement, based on an effective system of formative and summative assessment and linked to monitoring and evaluation (Figure 3).

A key concept underpinning *target setting* is the distinction between forecasts and targets. Forecasts are what a school, department or student might reasonably be expected to achieve anyway, based on what is known about students, and on trends in performance. Targets are forecasts with the addition of a modest or ambitious degree of challenge, to drive up standards.

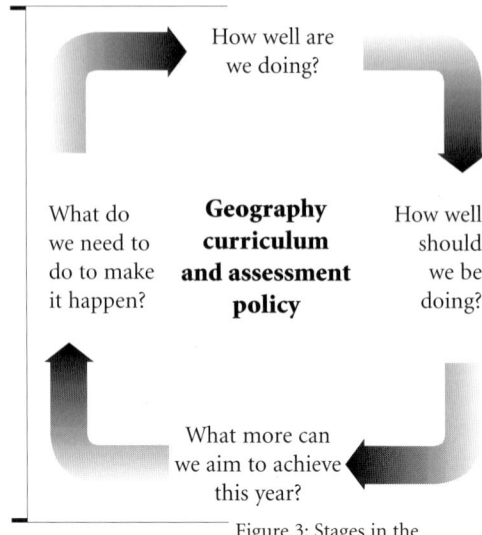

Figure 3: Stages in the improvement cycle.

It might seem that target setting is mainly a system of number crunching to establish grage or level targets, and several diagnostic or predictive systems, for examples YELLIS, are very effective in establishing these. However, it is important to emphasise, in setting targets for students, classes or year groups. Assessment gives teachers the information they need to set targets based in reality.

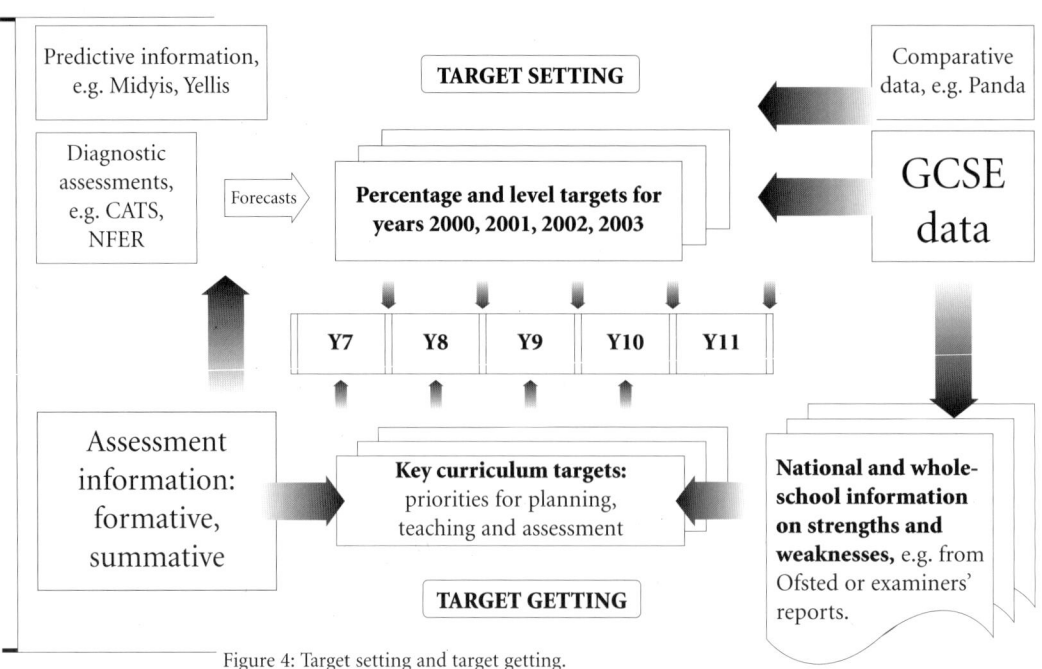

Figure 4: Target setting and target getting.

Target getting

Effective assessment, linked to monitoring and evaluation is also the key to *target getting* by teachers and students, turning grade or level targets into curriculum targets which identify strengths and weaknesses then closing these gaps. To emphasise the point, the process is far more than a data-gathering exercise; it is essential that it feeds into curriculum thange and non-numerical targets. Target setting without strategies for target getting is in danger of being a paper exercise. Figure 4 shows the central role played by assessment in both target setting, and target getting.

'Starting-point assessment' in year 7

Target setting has renewed interest in 'starting-point assessment in year 7' and the need to show 'added value' in the geography department. However, this assessment strategy needs careful handling if it is to be a meaningful experience for students, provide useful assessment information to help establish areas of strength and weakness, and set targets for progression.

One problem is that the wide range of geographical experience students bring from different schools means that it is difficult to assess what they have been taught. This is particularly so in urban schools where students arrive from large numbers of primary schools. A formal test of students' geographical skills, knowledge and understanding early in year 7 is likely to have limited success in assessing what they know, understand and can do. Both the teaching and assessment context in the new school may be unfamiliar to many. Remember too, that it is very difficult to make useful level judgements in relation to only a small part of the POS. Assessment in these circumstances is unlikely to allow students to show positive achievement and will therefore have little validity or reliability. It will provide weak evidence to support judgements about value added later in the key stage.

If we want to design a 'starting-point assessment' early in key stage 3, it will be more effective to base it on formative teacher assessment, as described in Chapter 4. It can be anchored by a rather more summative special 'assessment occasion', such as those outlined in Chapter 5, near the end of the first or second term. Organising assessment in this way will enable students to show what they know, understand and can do in relation to the taught curriculum in their new school. It will also help teachers to diagnose misconceptions and support students' learning, whilst providing good evidence of attainment to feed into the target setting process. The introductory unit of the QCA *Key Stage 3 Schemes of Work* 'Making connections' (QCA, 2000) presents a number of such assessment opportunities.

Summary

Strategies for setting short-term targets for improvement with students have been discussed in Chapter 4. Chapter 5 discusses the key role of feedback from regular in-depth assessments, linked perhaps with self-evaluation, to promote reflection and identify more substantial targets in the medium term. Chapter 7 has focused on longer term strategies, such as the use of examiners' reports and the results of end of key stage 3 moderation, to review attainment and focus on targets for improvement.

Professional development activities

1. Use the examiners' report for your GCSE syllabus to identify general strengths and weaknesses in geography. The most recent Ofsted report on national standards in geography may also be useful.
- Which strengths and weaknesses do you consider to be relevant to your department?
- What other information can you add, for example, from mock examinations or coursework moderation?
2. Now translate the weaknesses into key curriculum targets and identify the relevant medium-term (unit) plans where you need to take action.
3. Use Figure 4 to review the information you currently use to help you set targets. Are there any you need to reconsider or add?

Photo: Gary Cambers.

Chapter 8

Developing an assessment policy

- **What should a departmental assessment policy contain?**
- **Who is responsible for different aspects of assessment policy and practice?**

The main issues explored within this chapter are:

- **what an assessment policy is and what it should contain;**
- **strategies for developing a policy.**

Introduction

The purpose of an assessment policy is to formalise and codify practice and relate what we do and believe as a department to whole-school policy. It is an important reference point for members of the department, for other members of staff including those who occasionally teach geography and student teachers, and for fellow-professionals such as governors, advisers and inspectors. It is also good practice to ensure that students and parents are aware of the purposes of different aspects of assessment policy. Assessment policy is an important element in a departmental handbook, linking with other aspects such as curriculum planning and arrangements for monitoring, evaluation and target setting. Like these, the assessment policy should cover key stage 3, 14-16 and 16-18 courses.

'The best of the policies are specific about what will be assessed and when. They outline manageable procedures for recording and for using evidence of students' attainment. They derive from consistent and successful practice in the school and consequently carry the full support of the teachers' (Ofsted, 1998).

The departmental assessment policy

Figures 1 and 2 offer general advice about assessment policy and responsibilities for assessment.

Photo: Richard Greenhill.

A departmental policy on assessment may include guidelines on ways to:

- Plan for everyday assessment.

- Use assessment to inform the next steps in learning.

- Mark work and provide feedback to students.

- Record assessments.

- Use the outcomes from everyday assessment, and from SCAA's optional tests and tasks where used, to identify strengths and weaknesses and to inform the planning of future teaching.

- Report to parents on students' progress and on statutory assessments at the end of a key stage.

- Plan for the statutory assessments at the end of a key stage.

- Monitor and evaluate policies and procedures on assessment, recording and reporting.

A departmental assessment policy might also make clear that all teachers should be aware of:

- the purpose of assessment;

- equal opportunities, and how the policy will promote them;

- how assessment will be signalled in the planning;

- the value of coming to an agreed understanding of the standards set out in the national curriculum;

- the need to apply standards consistently when making judgements at the end of a key stage.

Heads of departments might:

- monitor teachers' marking and assessment practice in their school, subject or departments, and evaluate its effectiveness;

- support and monitor work within the department to promote consistency in assessments across their school, subject(s) or department;

- provide guidance to other teachers when statutory judgements are made;

- use the results of optional tests and tasks and teacher assessment to inform curriculum planning;

- liaise with the school assessment and special educational needs co-ordinators;

- when appropriate, liaise with other schools or take part in a local network, arranging the exchange of materials, visits or meetings.

Figure 1: Assessment policy guideline. Adapted from: SCAA, 1995.

Bishop Luffa School Geography Department

Assessment, recording and reporting in geography at key stage 3 consists of three integrated elements:

Element 1: The assessment and recording of students' work.

Element 2: The annual student profile.

Element 3: The recording and reporting of national curriculum levels of attainment.

When designing our assessment model we identified a number of core features which we wanted to incorporate. These were, in part, a response to the external constraints of the geography Order, but also reflected the school assessment policy as well as departmental needs. The structure which evolved allows us to:

	RESPONSIBILITIES	ISSUES	POSSIBLE STRATEGIES
Head of department	• Ensures that the department has clear and effective procedures for assessment. • Ensures that assessment procedures are being carried out. • Reviews the effectiveness of assessment. • Develops a scheme of work which shows learning objectives clearly. • Keeps under review the quality and impact of assessment. • Monitors marking. • Provides information about training opportunities available on assessment strategies. • Focuses on attainment within geography. • Monitors continuity and progression in geography. • Maintains assessment policy (including marking).	• How clearly are learning objectives articulated in teachers' short-term plans? • Are learning objectives appropriate for students of different abilities? • Is an appropriate range of assessment strategies being used? • Does marking in a subject give sufficient and accurate feedback to students? • How does a head of department know whether assessment procedures are effective? • How effectively are the outcomes of assessment being used?	• Develop a scheme of work with learning objectives showing expected standards at different ages. • Establish regular opportunities for teachers to discuss strategies for assessment. • Gather examples of students work to show how assessing students attainment leads to planning next steps. • Monitor teachers' short-term planning. • Monitor the progress of a sample of students with different abilities. • Establish a habit of teachers and students referring to learning objectives.
Teacher	• Ensures that all lessons have clear learning objectives appropriate to student's abilities. • Makes curriculum plans in the light of assessment. • Focuses on the attainment of individuals. • Keeps records of student's attainment.	• Are students aware of what they are intended to learn in each lesson? • Do students know the strengths and weaknesses of their work? • Are assessment strategies appropriate to planned learning objectives? • How do the outcomes of assessment inform the planning of next steps?	• Plan from what is known about student's attainment. • Tell students the purpose of each activity. • Be clear about how much of the student's work can be assessed during different lessons.

Figure 2: Responsibilities for assessment. Adapted from: SCAA, 1997.

- assess student attainment against *agreed criteria* accurately;
- *involve students* in the assessment and review of their own work;
- encourage *action planning* and *target setting;*
- *communicate* attainment, effort and progression to students, parents and school management effectively;
- *map* the progress of individual students and be able to compare them with whole class and year groups;
- *ensure continuity* in the teaching and assessment of student work by teachers;
- use assessment to *review the work of the department/teacher* in modifying schemes, styles and approaches to teaching.

Element 1: The assessment and recording of students' work

Figure 3 details the continuous assessment of students' work. The end product is the recording of grades and comments in the mark book, which is divided into sections that reflect the elements of the student profile shown in Figure 4 (Element 2).

Evidence for assessment

There are two main forms of evidence for assessment: students' work and core assessments.

EVIDENCE	STUDENT ROLE	TEACHER ROLE	CONTINUITY	RECORD
STUDENT WORK Exercise books Displays, etc. *Continuous*	*Students use symbols to self-assess work.* *Students record grades and merits on student record sheet in exercise books – providing a summary record of performance.*	*Work is assessed and graded for attainment and effort.* *Comments advise students about their performance – targets set to guide student progression.* *Teachers grade using criteria-referenced marking scheme.*	*Work is graded using agreed marking system.* *Standards agreed through discussion at departmental meetings, comments in syllabus and by reference to the portfolio of assessed student work.*	**MARK BOOK** Organised in sections for: Sense of Place Recall Understanding Enquiry General skills mapped for individuals and whole class. Merits and commendations recorded.
CORE ASSESSMENTS Criteria referenced assignments. Level descriptors of student performance use. *Twice per year*	*Students comment on performance, ease of working and set targets.* *Attainment and effort grades recorded in back of exercise book.* *Assignments kept by students – including detailed teacher comments.*	*Detailed comment on performance and targets for progress written using self-duplicating record sheet.* *Attainment and effort grades indicated for students.* *Levels recorded in mark book.*	*Standards agreed through discussion at departmental meetings, comments in syllabus and by reference to the portfolio of assessed student work.*	Copies of teacher/student comments retained.

Figure 3: Element 1: the assessment and recording of students' work.

Students' work

Students' work from exercise books, displays, etc., is graded according to the school/faculty marking scheme (on a scale A to D, plus a written effort comment). Comments about performance and targets for progression/improvement are also written in exercise books. These comments provide students with encouragement targeted to progression between national curriculum levels – although no reference to levels is specifically made. Such comments are not included on every piece of work – this would be both unrealistic and unnecessary. We aim to include comments of this type on every second or third piece of extended writing/more detailed work.

Students also make a record of their grades by filling in a record sheet in the back of their exercise books. In this way they are aware of their general level of performance and can easily identify areas of progress. They use symbols (smiley faces) at the end of key pieces of work to indicate how easy/difficult they found the task. This provides a valuable feedback to teachers which can be particularly helpful following more extended homework.

Underpinning all students' work is the school key stage scheme of work. This has been written to incorporate the national curriculum programme of study and includes key questions and guidance tied to

STUDENT ROLE		TEACHER ROLE
EXERCISE BOOKS *Review attainment and effort grades for work completed during the academic year.* *Read teacher comments written at end of some pieces of work.* *Review general presentation, etc.*	**JOINT REVIEW** Performance during the academic year is discussed. Overall standard of attainment and effort is identified and agreed. Action points and targets for continued student progression are identified.	**MARK BOOK** *Review attainment and effort grades for work marked during the academic year.* *Review record of skills and marks for sense of place.*
STUDENT RECORD SHEET *Review overall pattern of attainment as shown on the student record sheet in the back of the exercise book.*		**EXERCISE BOOKS** *Check through exercise books focusing upon teacher comments and general presentation/organisation.*
CORE ASSESSMENTS *Read teacher/student comments and targets for any core assessments completed.*		**CORE ASSESSMENTS** *Read teacher/student comments and targets for any core assessments completed.*

STUDENT PROFILE

Overall performance/attainment graded for:

Sense of place, recall, understanding, enquiry/investigations and, general effort.

Comment *and* **action points** *written by* **student.** *Focus on strengths/weaknesses and areas for future action.*

Teacher comment *with focus on strengths/ weaknesses and suggestions for future progress.*

Figure 4: Element 2 – student profile.

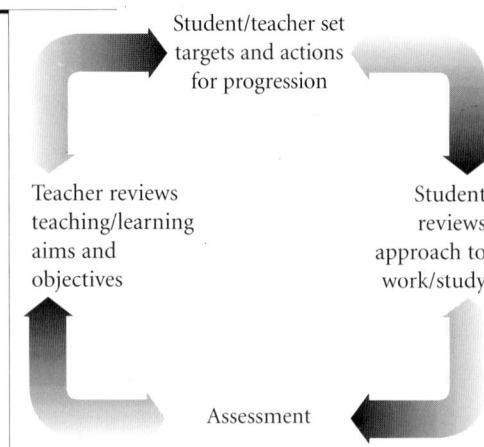

Student/teacher set
targets and actions
for progression

Teacher reviews
teaching/learning
aims and
objectives

Student
reviews
approach to
work/study

Assessment

Figure 5: The cycle of assessment and review.

the level descriptions. It forms an essential part of the assessment package, since the student exercise book is one of the artefacts used to assess levels (see Element 3). If students are not given access to particular topics and styles of work, or are not encouraged to write about or explain relationships in an extended form, evidence for attainment at higher levels will not be easily identified within the course of everyday work.

A regular feature of departmental meetings is discussion of the scheme of work and agreeing the focus of extended written work. This combines with the specific detail included in the scheme of work to provide continuity between teachers and contributes to the development of clear, shared standards and expectations.

'Core assessments'

The second main form of evidence consists of the 'core assessments'. These are designed to assess a variety of topics at a range of national curriculum levels. Each task is criterion-referenced and is assessed using level descriptors. Each assignment is undertaken by the whole cohort and, typically, two such core assessments are set in each year of key stage 3.

Element 2: Student profile

Figure 4 shows how a variety of sources of evidence are reviewed to build up a student's profile.

The importance of review

Throughout the assessment process, student and teacher review and target setting is highlighted. Figure 5 illustrates how review by teachers and students is essential for development and progression.

Written comments, grades and discussion with teachers enable students to review their performance and adjust their working and study methods. Action plans for improvement and progress cannot develop without this supported self-assessment. Similarly, teachers review and adjust their teaching aims and learning objectives as a result of analysing student performance.

Element 3: Assessing and recording levels and mapping progression

Tracking progression

Each student has a progression sheet which follows him or her though key stage 3. It is designed to record level judgements against the four aspects of attainment, gradually map them across the key stage and set a yearly target. The transfer information from primary schools is attached to each progression sheet. At the end of year 9, the progression sheet is used with other evidence to allocate an end-of-key stage level of attainment for geography. This is recorded on the progression sheet, which will then be transferred into year 10. Figure 6 shows the annual cycle of assessment, recording and review which guides progression through key stage 3.

Professional development activities

1. Study Figures 1 and 2. Use them as a checklist of your own departmental policy. Which sections would you think of developing or adding to your existing policy?

2. Read your own policy again, from the point of view of a governor or visitor to the department. Are there any aspects which you would like to find out more about, or which could be clearer?

JANUARY

EVIDENCE	CONTINUITY	RECORD

MARK BOOK

Look at range of skills assessed as satisfactory.

Review grades.

EXERCISE BOOKS

Review work to date, comments and targets set.

Standards are agreed through discussion at departmental meetings, comments in syllabus and by reference to the portfolio of assessed student work.

Tick boxes to show skills attainment.

Indicate current performance and levels for the national curriculum strands.

Indicate current overall level.

Date and initial.

CORE ASSESSMENTS

Review comments and grades of any core assessments completed.

DEPARTMENT DATABASE

Current overall national curriculum levels are transferred to the departmental database.

This allows individuals to be compared with the key stage cohort as well as enabling ranking/mapping of the key stage cohort.

JULY

EVIDENCE	CONTINUITY	RECORD

MARK BOOK

Look at range of skills assessed as satisfactory.

Review grades.

EXERCISE BOOKS

Review work to date, comments and targets set.

Standards are agreed through discussion at departmental meetings, comments in syllabus and by reference to the portfolio of assessed student work.

Tick boxes to show skills attainment.

Indicate current performance and levels for the national curriculum strands.

Indicate current overall level.

Date and initial.

CORE ASSESSMENTS

Review comments and grades of any core assessments completed.

PROFILE

Review profile grades, comments and action plans.

DEPARTMENT DATABASE

Current overall national curriculum levels are transferred to the departmental database.

This allows individuals to be compared with the key stage cohort as well as enabling ranking/mapping of the key stage cohort.

Figure 6: A yearly assessment cycle.

References

ACAC (1996) *Consistency in Teacher Assessment: Exemplification of Standards, Geography, Key Stage 3.* Cardiff: ACAC.

ACAC (1997) *Consistency in Teacher Assessment: Optional Tests and Tasks – Key Stage 3 Geography.* Cardiff: ACAC.

Balderstone, D. and Lambert, D. (1992) *Assessment Matters.* Sheffield: Geographical Association.

Battersby, J., Webster, A. and Younger, M. (1995) *The Case Study in GCSE Geography: Experiences from the Avery Hill Project.* Cardiff: WJEC.

Bennetts, T. (1995) 'Continuity and progression', *Teaching Geography,* 20, 2, pp. 75-9.

Black, P. and Wiliam, D. (1998) *Inside the Black Box: Raising standards through classroom assessment.* London: School of Education, Kings College.

Butt, G. and Smith, P. (1998) 'Educational standards and assessment in geography – some cause for concern?', *Teaching Geography,* 23, 3, pp. 147-9.

Butt, G., Lambert, D. and Telfer, S. (1995) *Assessment Works: Approaches to assessment in geography at key stages 1, 2 and 3.* Sheffield: Geographical Association.

Dearing, R. (1995) *The National Curriculum and its Assessment.* London: SCAA.

Dearing, R. in SCAA (1996a) *Consistency in Teacher Assessment: Exemplification of Standards – Key Stage 3 Geography.* London: SCAA.

GAIN (no date) *Assessment, Recording and Reporting.* Sheffield: Geographical Association, Geography Advisers and Inspectors Network.

Gipps, (1994) *Beyond Testing: Towards a theory of educational assessment.* London: Falmer.

Harlen, W., Gipps, C., Broadfoot, P. and Nuttall, D. (1992) 'Assessment and the improvement of education', *The Curriculum Journal,* 3, 3, pp. 215-30.

James, M. (1998) *Using Assessment for School Improvement.* Oxford: Heinemann.

Jones, B. (1999) 'Curriculum continuity in geography', *Teaching Geography,* 24, 1, pp. 5-9.

Lambert, D. (1996) 'Assessing pupils' attainment and supporting learning' in Kent, A., Lambert, D., Naish, M. and Slater, F. (eds) *Geography in Education: Viewpoints on teaching and learning.* Cambridge: Cambridge University Press, pp. 260-87.

Lambert, D. (1997) 'Principles of pupil assessment' in Tilbury, D. and Williams, M. (eds) *Teaching and Learning in Geography.* London: Routledge, pp. 255-65.

Ofsted (1995) *The Ofsted Handbook: Guidance on the inspection of secondary schools.* London: HMSO.

Ofsted (1998) *Teacher Assessment in the Core Subjects at Key Stage 2: Policy and practice.* London: The Stationery Office.

Ofsted (1999) *Standards in the Secondary Curriculum 1997/98.* London: The Stationery Office.

Qualifications and Curriculum Authority (QCA) (1998) *Geographical Enquiry at Key Stages 1-3.* London: QCA.

QCA (2000) *Key Stage 3 Scheme of Work: Geography.* London: QCA.

Rawling, E and Westaway, J (1996) 'Progression and assessment in geography at key stage 3', *Teaching Geography,* 21, 3, pp. 123-8.

SCAA (1995) *Consistency in Teacher Assessment: Guidance for schools, key stages 1-3.* London: SCAA.

SCAA (1996a) *Consistency in Teacher Assessment: Exemplification of standards – geography key stage 3.* London: SCAA.

SCAA (1996b) *Consistency in Teacher Assessment: Optional tests and tasks (key stage 3) geography.* London: SCAA.

SCAA (1997a) *Expectations in Geography at Key Stages 1 and 2.* London: SCAA.

SCAA (1997b) *Teacher Assessment in Key Stage 2.* London: SCAA.

TGAT (1988) *Task Group on Assessment and Testing: A report.* London: DES.

Tidmarsh, C. and Weeden, P. (1997) 'Using optional tests and tasks', *Teaching Geography,* 22, 2, pp. 71-6.

Westaway, J. and Rawling, E. (1997) 'Preparing for statutory assessment at key stage 3', *Teaching Geography,* 22, 1, pp. 40-1.

Wiegand. P. (1997)'Assessment in the primary school' in Tilbury, D. and Williams, M. (eds) *Teaching and Learning in Geography.* London: Routledge, pp. 266-74.